THE FORT PITT BLOCK HOUSE

THE FORT PITT BLOCK HOUSE

EMILY M. WEAVER

with the Fort Pitt Society of the Daughters of the American Revolution

THE History PRESS

Published by The History Press
Charleston, SC 29403
www.historypress.net

Back cover: Bottom photo by Roy Engelbrecht.

First published 2013

Manufactured in the United States

ISBN 978.1.60949.933.4

Library of Congress CIP data applied for.

Notice: The information in this book is true and complete to the best of our knowledge. It is offered without guarantee on the part of the author or The History Press. The author and The History Press disclaim all liability in connection with the use of this book.

This publication is dedicated to those early women of the Fort Pitt Society of the Daughters of the American Revolution who fought railroads, industrialists and politicians to save the Fort Pitt Block House from destruction and who worked relentlessly for its preservation. It is from their efforts that we still have a little piece of history standing today.

Contents

Preface

This book is meant to serve as a complete history of Pittsburgh's oldest architectural landmark, the Fort Pitt Block House. The Block House was constructed in 1764 as a defensive redoubt for Fort Pitt, a major British fort during the eighteenth century. It sits at the historic Forks of the Ohio River (also known as "the Point") in Pittsburgh, Pennsylvania. Not only is it the oldest building in Pittsburgh, but it is also the oldest authenticated structure in western Pennsylvania and the oldest British structure west of the Allegheny Mountains.

The Block House survived the eventual demolition of Fort Pitt through its reuse as a residence. The building served as a house to countless families from circa 1785 to 1894—more than 100 years! Beginning in 1894, the Block House became privately owned and operated by the Fort Pitt Society of the Daughters of the American Revolution of Allegheny County, a supporting organization of the Pittsburgh Chapter of the National Society of the Daughters of the American Revolution. The organization restored the Block House to its original appearance and opened it to the public as a historical site and museum. During the early days of the society's ownership, the Block House became threatened by the Pennsylvania Railroad as it sought to expand its properties over the site of the historic structure. The Fort Pitt Society fought the railroad company for many years until 1907, when a state law was passed prohibiting the building's destruction. The Block House still stands in its original location, surrounded by modern-day Point State Park near downtown Pittsburgh. It has been open to the public for nearly 120 years.

PREFACE

When guests visit the Block House today, many ask for a book or some kind of publication covering the history of the structure. Disappointment usually follows when they are told that there is no such publication. Although there is a vast number of works on the history of Fort Pitt, there is nothing focusing solely on the history of the Block House. To be sure, many books and articles mention the building either through a small chapter, a brief paragraph or a simple sentence. These references, however, do not include the entire history of the building or even an accurate history.

This leads to the next purpose of this book, which is to give the most accurate and knowledgeable account of this fascinating structure. What little exists of formally published information about the Block House is prone to errors and a lack of research. It should be stated, of course, that to a certain extent, much of what is now known about the Block House has been made possible through recent advances in archaeology and preservation work, as well as the wider availability of documents for research. Also, not everything that is important to the building's story today was important in the past. A perfect example of this is the Block House's former use as a dwelling, a major part of its history that has largely been overlooked or dismissed by past historians.

A final purpose for this publication is celebration. The Block House will turn 250 years old in 2014, and events are being planned to commemorate this anniversary milestone. Through celebrating the 250th anniversary of the Block House, the people of Pittsburgh and its surrounding areas will essentially be celebrating their earliest beginnings. The Fort Pitt Block House symbolizes the history that happened here long ago when French, British and American Indian cultures clashed during the eighteenth century. It also serves as a monument to the test of time—a time that at various moments was quite turbulent for the Block House. It is a true witness to history, and its constant presence is a reminder of all of the events that took place in Pittsburgh over the last 250 years.

Acknowledgements

This book would not have been possible without the assistance of numerous individuals and organizations. I would like to acknowledge the following for their generosity in providing images and research assistance for this publication: Miriam Meislik of the University of Pittsburgh Archives Service Center, Gil Pietrzak of the Pennsylvania Department at the Carnegie Library of Pittsburgh, Greg Priore of the Special Collections Room at the Carnegie Library of Pittsburgh, Elizabeth Roark and Rachel Grove Rohrbaugh of Chatham University, Theresa Rea and Art Louderback of the Detre Library & Archives at the Senator John Heinz History Center and Alan Gutchess and the staff of the Fort Pitt Museum.

Although I spent many months reading and researching all things Block House, much of the groundwork for this research had already been laid by my predecessor, Kelly Linn. I deeply appreciate all that Kelly has done with her past studies of the Block House, as well as the assistance she provided me during the writing of this work. I am also grateful to the following for their help with this book, whether through research, proofreading or simply lending assistance when needed: Jessica Cox, Donna Knechtel-Paszek, Joanne Ostergaard, Maureen Mahoney Hill and Molly Fuchs. My family must also be acknowledged for their unfailing support and encouragement throughout the researching and writing of this book, especially my husband, Jim, who spent many evenings listening to story after story of the Fort Pitt Block House.

Finally, I would like to thank all of the members of the Fort Pitt Society of the Daughters of the American Revolution of Allegheny County

(Pittsburgh Chapter NSDAR) for allowing me to write this book about their treasured building. It is a story that needed to be told, and it would not have been possible without their support. Thank you.

Prologue

The French and Indian War, Fort Pitt and Pontiac's Rebellion

As stated in the preface to this book, the Block House was originally built as a defensive redoubt for a British fortification named Fort Pitt. Although the building was constructed in 1764, its origins are part of a much larger story beginning over ten years prior to that time. It is the story of the struggle between France and Britain for control of the eastern half of North America; of the failed efforts of a native people, the North American Indians, to retain their lands and rights from encroaching Europeans; and of the beginning of a new city, Pittsburgh.

War for Empire

The French and Indian War—or Seven Years' War, as it was known in Europe—officially lasted from 1756 to 1763 and was one of the earliest global conflicts in world history. Beginning as a squabble in the foothills of the Allegheny Mountains of modern-day western Pennsylvania, it ended as a major war with battle scenes on the European continent as well as far-off India. This war would cast Britain as the most powerful empire in the world, as well as the dominant colonial force in North America.

During the eighteenth century, the Forks of the Ohio River, now Pittsburgh, Pennsylvania, was an area of vast importance to many different nations and people. It was home to American Indians such as the Delaware,

Shawnee and Mingo tribes, collectively known as the Ohio Indians. These tribes fought for their autonomy from the powerful neighboring nation of the Iroquois Confederacy of Six Nations throughout the seventeenth and eighteenth centuries.[1] The Forks of the Ohio was also important to another powerful nation, France, whose colonies in North America encompassed Canada, the Illinois Country and New Orleans. The Ohio River Valley, located west of the Allegheny Mountains, served as a potential connector for New France's far-flung colonies, as well as an area in which to extend their trade to the native tribes. Another empire that found the Ohio River Valley to be of great interest was the British empire. The British colonies of North America were much closer together than those of New France but were largely located east of the Appalachian Mountain ranges. The wave of migration to the English colonies pushed for westward expansion beginning in the eighteenth century. British colonial officials and residents looked directly to areas such as the Forks of the Ohio as places to expand their settlements and, much like the French, extend their trade with American Indians. Finally, within the realm of the British empire, there was fighting among the colonies over who had jurisdiction in the western areas. Virginia and Pennsylvania, in particular, were at odds with each other over who had the rights to control the Ohio River Valley, which happened to border both of their domains.[2]

The large area encompassing the Forks and the Ohio River Valley began to be hotly contested by the French and the British as early as the late 1740s. Around this time, English traders and fur trappers were encroaching on the Ohio River in an effort to compete with the massive trading between the French and the Native American Indians. It was also during this time that the British began to form land companies in order to capitalize on the development of the Ohio Territory, as well as its lucrative trading empire. One such company, the Ohio Land Company, was formed in 1747 by Virginian landowners. Their primary focus was to develop all of the territory west of the Allegheny Mountains by selling it to settlers and speculators hungry for land. The only problem with this plan, of course, was the French. By 1749, the company had begun to build fortified storehouses below the Forks of the Ohio in the Virginia territories.[3] In response to the increasing advances by British traders and land companies, the French launched an expedition from Montreal in 1749 led by Céloron de Blainville. During this expedition, lead plates were buried at various locations throughout the Ohio River Valley, thereby claiming ownership of the valley and its environs. By 1753, they had constructed three forts in what is now western Pennsylvania, including Fort de la Presque Isle (present-day Erie) along

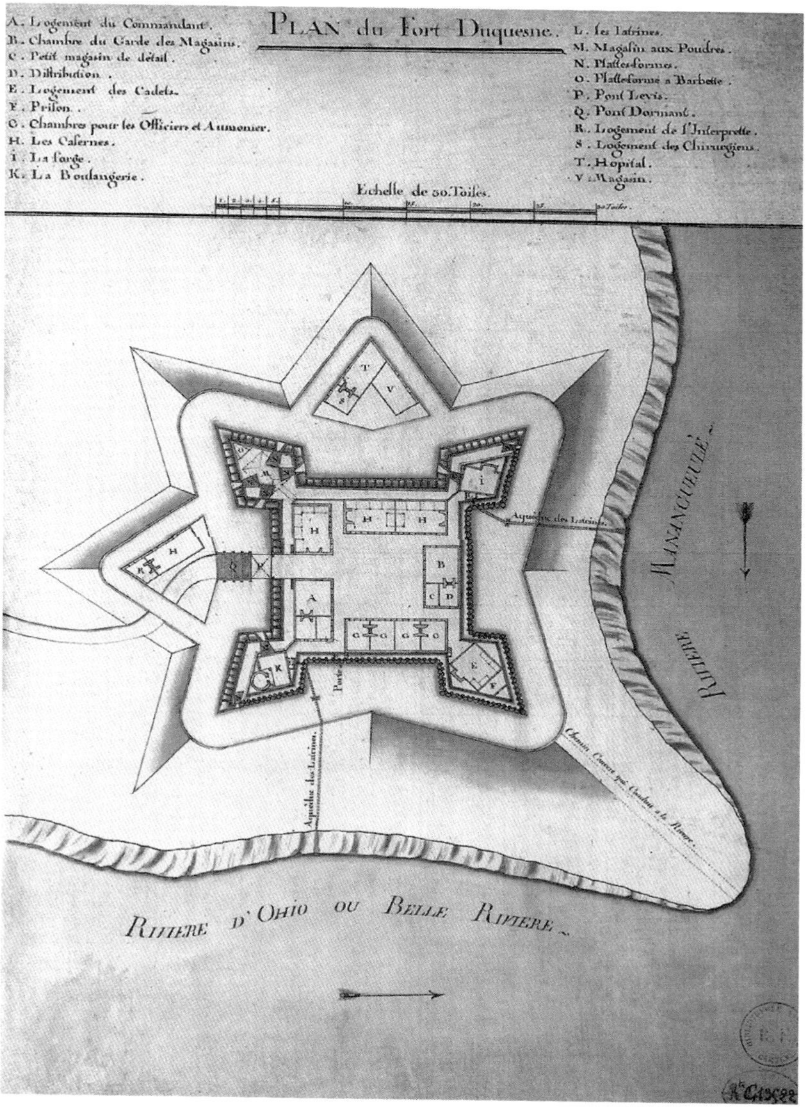

The plan of Fort Duquesne, the French fort that stood at the Forks of the Ohio from 1754 to 1758. *From a drawing in the Bibliothèquenationale de France.*

the shore of Lake Erie, Fort LeBoeuf (present-day Waterford) near French Creek and Fort Machault (present-day Franklin) at the confluence of French Creek and the Allegheny River. A fourth fortification was planned for the forks of the Ohio River, the place where the Allegheny and Monongahela Rivers meet to form the mighty Ohio.[4]

An engraving depicting men from General Braddock's campaign of 1755 overlooking the site of Fort Duquesne at the Point. *From* Old Fort Duquesne *(1873).*

The completion of the French fortifications led the governor of Virginia (who was also a member of the Ohio Company) to send an emissary to Fort LeBoeuf to tell the French that they had to stop their construction and leave the territory. This emissary, a young George Washington, left in the early winter of 1753, passing by the Forks of the Ohio (also called "the Point" due to the land pointing out toward the Ohio River) on his way up to Fort LeBoeuf. The mission ended in failure for the British as the French refused to leave what they thought rightfully belonged to them. Virginia instantly responded to the French by sending a small army of provincial troops up to the Forks of the Ohio in January–February 1754. Led by Captain William Trent, an agent of the Ohio Land Company, they were given the task of constructing a small fortification at the Point of the Forks to be called Fort Prince George (better known as Trent's Fort).[5]

Trent was unable to complete his fort due to the oncoming French army down the Allegheny River. It reached the Point in April 1754, forcing Trent and his small group of men into surrender. Now the French had control of the Forks, and to solidify this control, they built Fort Duquesne, named after the governor of New France. The British made two initial attempts to regain control of the Point. The first of these attempts was led by George Washington under the auspices of Virginia in May 1754. He and his men encountered a small group of French soldiers led by Ensign Joseph Coulon de Villiers de Jumonville near modern-day Uniontown, Pennsylvania. A skirmish ensued resulting in the death of Jumonville. This event is largely considered to be the first bloodshed of the French and Indian War, although war was not declared until two years later. In the following months, Washington and his men were counterattacked at nearby Fort Necessity. Although he survived, Washington had to retreat back to Virginia in defeat. The second attempt by the British resulted in the humiliating defeat of General Edward Braddock in 1755. Braddock, a British general, led a vast army of British regular troops and provincial troops up from Virginia toward the Forks of the Ohio, only to be soundly defeated by the French and their Native American allies at the mouth of Turtle Creek on the Monongahela River, a few miles south of Fort Duquesne.[6]

ENTER FORT PITT

War had officially been declared between Britain and France by 1756; however, the British were not able to make another attempt to take over Fort Duquesne until 1758. By this time, the British secretary of state, William Pitt, had begun to plan a three-pronged attack on the French in North America. One of the three plans involved the capture of Fort Duquesne. Led by General John Forbes, the British army began a lengthy campaign, marching from Philadelphia to the Forks of the Ohio. The Forbes Campaign reached British Fort Ligonier in the summer of 1758, located less than fifty miles east of Fort Duquesne.[7]

Pittsburgh and Fort Pitt were named after William Pitt the Elder, the British secretary of state at the time of the Forbes Campaign. He was also known as the Earl of Chatham. *From* Fort Duquesne and Fort Pitt *(1899)*.

Forbes planned his campaign very carefully and chose to proceed slowly. This caused impatience among his men, particularly with Major James Grant. Grant, one of the first to arrive at Fort Ligonier, decided to take eight hundred men from the Seventy-seventh (Scottish Highlanders) and strike out for Fort Duquesne ahead of the larger army being led by Forbes. Grant and his men reached the Point in September 1758, whereupon they were soundly defeated by the French. Despite this defeat, Forbes proceeded onward toward Ligonier, arriving shortly thereafter. Although on the heels of victory, the French decided to burn down Fort Duquesne and flee the area in the face of Forbes's oncoming army. When Forbes and his men arrived at the Point on November 24, 1758, they found the smoldering ruins of Fort Duquesne (as well as the decomposing bodies of Grant's Highlanders).[8]

Now that the British had a firm control over the Forks of the Ohio and its surrounding areas, they began to build one of the largest and most elaborate fortifications in North America, Fort Pitt, which was named for William Pitt by John Forbes, who called the Point and its environs "Pittsburgh."[9] The fort was constructed between 1759 and 1761, and it was located on the Point, although it was not built directly on top of the site of Fort Duquesne. Fort Pitt was pentagonal in shape, with five bastions reaching out from its corners—the Monongahela Bastion and Flag Bastion facing the Monongahela River (west and south), the Ohio/Lower Bastion and Music Bastion facing the Allegheny River (north and northeast) and the Grenadier Bastion facing the land directly (southeast). The majority of its bastions, ramparts and curtain walls were of earthen or dirt construction. Forts consisting of such construction materials proved resilient against most cannon fire and, if well maintained, could stand for a considerable amount of time. Because the British feared an attack from the land more so than the water, Fort Pitt's land-based walls were faced with a brick revetment that extended from the tip of the Flag Bastion, encompassing the Grenadier Bastion, to the tip of the Music Bastion. This revetment especially could protect the fort from cannon attacks.[10]

Fort Pitt was completed by the end of 1761, being built to withstand attacks from the French and their Native American allies. The fort's first attack, however, was not made by the cannons and mortars of the French nor by the musket fire of the Indians. It was made by the flooded waters of the three rivers surrounding Fort Pitt. Two major floods devastated the fort and its environs within the first two years of its existence. The first flood, occurring on January 9, 1762, created excessive damage to its earthen ramparts and walls, which were not sodded properly when constructed. Colonel Henry Bouquet, the commandant of Fort Pitt at this time, provided the following description of the flood:

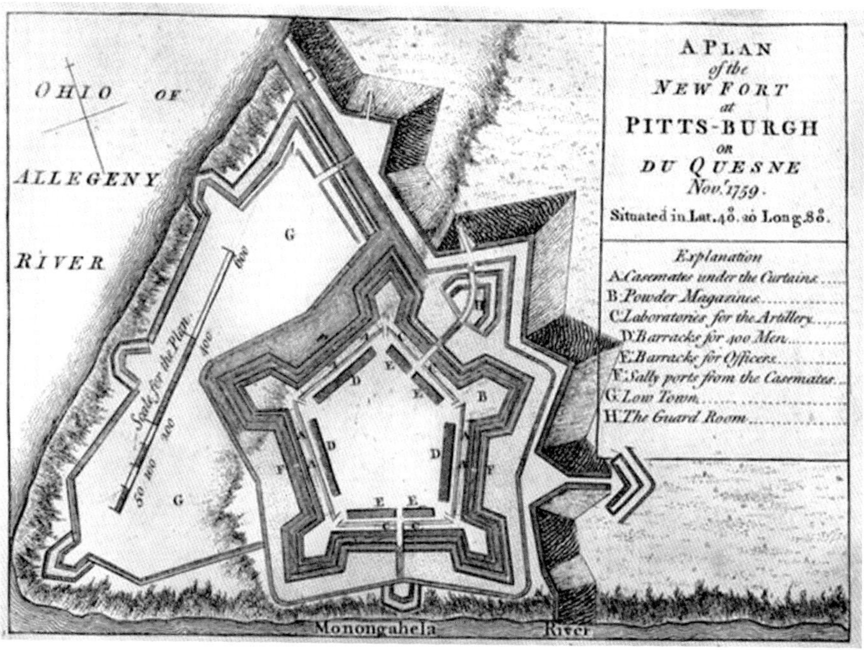

A 1759 plan of the new British fort planned at Pittsburgh, Fort Pitt. The fort was eventually completed in 1761. *From John Rocque's* A Set of Plans and Forts in America *(1765).*

> *The 9th the Rivers run 10 Feet over the Banks, which had not happened at any flood since this Place is built...The Water came upon us thro' the Drains, Gate, and Sally Ports, and boiled in large Springs out of the ground in Several Parts of the Fort...The 11th we could discover Part of our Disasters. All the Sod Work done last year, and great Part of the Year before tumbled down upon the Piquets, and a good deal of Earth washed away. The Courtin* [sic] *on the Monongahela, finished two years ago, has Suffered less, tho' Part of the Sods are gone.*[11]

The Ohio Bastion suffered significant damage as well, it being situated at a lower level than the other bastions. The brick revetment on the land side bore the brunt of the currents, thereby saving Fort Pitt from total destruction. The second flood hit the fort on March 11, 1763, cresting twenty-two inches higher than the previous flood. Although the garrison was better prepared for the Flood of 1763, and though the flood itself did not cause as much damage as before, the fort was now in a very vulnerable state. The flood damages sustained by the fortification were never repaired and would later serve as a contributing factor to the fort's demolition.[12]

PONTIAC'S WAR AND THE SIEGE OF FORT PITT

Unfortunately for the garrison at Pittsburgh, the Flood of 1763 was quickly followed by the worst man-made attack the fort would ever see: the Siege of Fort Pitt. The French and Indian War officially ended in February 1763 with the Treaty of Paris, but the French had ceased to be a threat to the Forks of the Ohio as early as 1760. Contrastingly, the Ohio Indians actually increased as a threat to all British forts and settlements west of the Allegheny Mountains, culminating in an uprising called Pontiac's War. Beginning in the spring of 1763, Pontiac's War was a large and deadly rebellion led by American Indians from as far west as Fort Detroit against the British. The Siege of Fort Pitt, which lasted throughout the summer of 1763, was a significant part of this rebellion.

Prior to the rebellion, a conference was held in Easton, Pennsylvania, in October 1758 as an attempt to make peace with the Ohio nations, particularly the Delaware tribes. The resulting treaty was a success in that it virtually set aside those lands west of the Allegheny Mountains for the Ohio Indians; however, it still allowed for Iroquois dominance over those tribes. Despite the fact that the Iroquois still held control, and despite the prevailing fear of white settlement on their lands, the Indians allowed the British to continue their march and the construction of forts in the West in order to defeat the French.[13] The Easton treaty, coupled with the fall of Fort Duquesne by November 1758, caused many Native Americans in the Ohio Territory to switch to the side of the British for the remainder of the French and Indian War. Although the French were now defeated, the British continued to construct forts and other outposts throughout the Ohio Territory over the next five years. With the fortifications came white settlement from the East, pouring into the new land. This settlement and the increase of fortifications caused major concern for the Ohio Indians, and their concern began to grow into anger.[14]

Not only were the Ohio Indians becoming increasingly frustrated over the growing presence of the British, but they were also becoming frustrated by the actions of the commander in chief of the British forces in North America: General Jeffrey Amherst. Amherst had little understanding or tolerance of American Indian cultures and societies. Given the task of reducing expenditures in the North American colonies, he prohibited the practice of gift-giving to the Indians, a practice that had been followed for more than a century by both French and British governments. Gift-giving was essential to Indian trade and negotiations; not only did it serve in maintaining peaceful relations, but it also

This watercolor by Richard Schlecht depicts Fort Pitt and its surrounding village as it may have appeared shortly after its completion in 1761. *Courtesy of the Fort Pitt Museum, Pennsylvania Historical and Museum Commission.*

provided Native Americans with highly desired supplies such as ammunitions, tools and rum. The Ohio Indians had become so dependent on this trade and gift-giving that to end it was to threaten the peace of the frontier, where British and Indian lives were at stake.[15]

A wave of discontent among American Indians stretched from the Forks of the Ohio out to Fort Detroit in the West. Feeding off of this restlessness, Indian leaders began to emerge, including Guyasuta, Neolin and Pontiac. As early as 1761, Guyasuta, a Mingo chief from the Ohio Territory, began to push for an uprising—even going so far as to rally the support of the Great Lakes Indians around Fort Detroit. Neolin, a Delaware chief and self-proclaimed prophet, also began to foment rebellion by encouraging other Indians to dispose of white ways and return to native lifestyles prior to European settlement.[16] Both Guyasuta and Neolin influenced Pontiac, an Ottawa chief from the Great Lakes, whose calls for war against the British proved to be the tipping point.

Talk of rebellion had become reality by May 9, 1763, with the siege of Fort Detroit, led by Pontiac. The Ohio Indians took up the hatchet and began to take siege of Fort Pitt as early as May 28, 1763. At the start of the siege, Fort Pitt was still in heavy disrepair from flooding, with only 145 men in its garrison and a low supply of flour and other necessities. The fort and its surroundings received constant threats and attacks from Indians over the next two months. Captain Simeon Ecuyer, placed in command of the fort, wrote the following shortly after the attacks began: "I think the uprising is general; I tremble for our posts. I think according to reports that I am surrounded by Indians."[17] By June the British forts of Venango (formerly Machault), LeBoeuf and Presque Isle had been taken over by the Indians and burned to the ground. Settlers across the frontier witnessed the destruction of their homes and the violent deaths of their families. General Amherst finally felt compelled to send relief to Fort Pitt in early June 1763. The man sent on this mission was Colonel Henry Bouquet.[18]

Colonel Henry Bouquet was born in Rolle, Switzerland, in 1719. Enlisting as a cadet at the age of seventeen, Bouquet began his military career fighting in the War for Austrian Succession and serving in the Swiss Guards for Holland. In 1755, as Britain began to search for suitable men to train and lead their troops in North America, Bouquet was recruited as a lieutenant colonel for the new Sixtieth Regiment of Foot, the Royal Americans. Arriving in North America by 1756, he became known as a reliable and capable officer with a talent for frontier warfare. Fluent in French and English, he played an influential role as General Forbes's second in command during the campaign of 1758 to capture Fort Duquesne.[19]

Bouquet was placed in command of Fort Pitt toward the end of 1760, witnessing the final phases of construction for the fort as well as the devastation of the Flood of 1762. He continued at Fort Pitt until the end of 1762, when he decided to take up his winter quarters in Philadelphia. Prior to leaving for the East, Bouquet placed Captain Simeon Ecuyer in charge of the fort; Ecuyer was therefore in command during both the Flood of 1763 and the Siege of Fort Pitt.[20] Although Ecuyer and Bouquet kept in constant contact through letters, it had become apparent to Bouquet that he was badly needed at Pittsburgh. Due to the attacks from the Native Americans, the families and other inhabitants surrounding Fort Pitt were forced to take shelter within its walls, leaving the fort heavily crowded and polluted. Added to these conditions were the diminishing supplies of staples such as flour and meat. Bouquet not only had to stop the attacks on Fort Pitt, but he had to keep its inhabitants from starvation as well.

After spending weeks trying to gather supplies and men, Bouquet set off from Philadelphia on June 25, 1763. Amherst gave Bouquet nearly five hundred men to fulfill his mission, including the Royal Americans and two Highland regiments from Scotland—the Forty-second Regiment "Black Watch" and the Seventy-seventh Regiment of Montgomery's Highlanders. Stopping at Carlisle to gather more supplies, Bouquet finally left for Fort Pitt on July 15 with a mixture of Scottish Highlanders, Royal Americans (many of whom were German) and civilian teamsters. Many of the Scottish troops were sick with malaria after just returning from campaigns in the

West Indies. This illness, combined with the summer heat and bad roads, caused for slow movement of Bouquet and his convoy.[21]

This early rendition of Colonel Henry Bouquet is copied from a painting by John Wollaston. Bouquet, known mainly for his victory at the Battle of Bushy Run in 1763, is credited with the construction of the Fort Pitt Block House. *From* Fort Duquesne and Fort Pitt *(1899)*.

Meanwhile, back at Fort Pitt, the Indians gathered at the fort on July 26 in an effort to negotiate with the British for an end to the fighting. They asked for the British to leave their forts and return to the East, as the Forks of the Ohio and its environs belonged to the Indians. Their request was thrown out by Captain Ecuyer, thus ending a chance for peace. Intense fighting picked up as the Indians renewed their attack on the fort. Attacks on Fort Pitt continued until August 1, when the Indians stopped firing and left the area, heading east. The Ohio Indians had captured one of Bouquet's couriers, reading his message that Bouquet was on his way to relieve Fort Pitt. Faced with the decision of either waiting at the fort for Bouquet and his men to arrive or surprising the army with an attack en route, the Indians ultimately decided to intercept Bouquet as he made his way west.[22]

Reaching Fort Ligonier on August 2, Bouquet and his troops rested for a few days and then continued on their journey. Because of his courier being intercepted, Bouquet had a great suspicion that the Indians could attack at any moment while on the march to Fort Pitt. On August 5, his men neared Bushy Run, a midway point between Forts Ligonier and Pitt. On that morning, the ambush Bouquet had suspected occurred. Lasting into the next day, the fighting was intense on both sides, but it became evident that the Indians could very well win if Bouquet did not come up with a strategy. Thinking quickly, Bouquet decided to pretend that he and his men were retreating from the battlefield, allowing for the Indians to come out into the open. This act of deception proved successful, and Bouquet was able to soundly defeat the Ohio Indians and relieve Fort Pitt as a result of the Battle of Bushy Run. Colonel Bouquet entered the gates of Fort Pitt on the evening of August 10 as a hero of the frontier.[23]

Chapter 1

The Building of the Fort Pitt Block House

I have caused Three Redoubts to be built...

The Siege of Fort Pitt of 1763 would prove to be the worst and last attack that the fort would ever witness. Following the return of Colonel Bouquet, life at the fort and in the surrounding areas began to quiet down and return to a sort of normalcy. Despite this sense of peace, Bouquet still thought it best to make some repairs and changes to Fort Pitt and its defense. The damages caused by the Floods of 1762 and 1763 were never completely repaired, and the sides of the fort facing toward the three rivers were in most need of extra defensive measures. On December 27, 1763, Bouquet wrote the following to his new commanding officer, General Thomas Gage:

> *Three Sides of this Fort which are not reveted having been rendered almost defenceless* [sic] *by Two successive Floods in 1762, and 1763, I have caused Three Redoubts to be built on the glacis, to cover them. Two are completed, and the Third going on, as fast as the Weather will permit.*[24]

One of the three redoubts mentioned in the quote is the building now known as the Fort Pitt Block House. Before going into the actual construction of the Block House and the other redoubts, a brief overview of redoubts in general and their function in eighteenth-century fortifications is necessary. The term *redoubt* is derived from Medieval Latin as a "secret place," although by the eighteenth century, it was a word used to define a specific type of

An early twentieth-century drawing of the Block House as it may have looked in about 1764. *From* The Common School Catalogue *(1906).*

military structure used as part of larger fortifications. Redoubts were mostly built in North America throughout the seventeenth, eighteenth and nineteenth centuries. They could be placed close to a fort's walls, or they could be placed in the outer defense works of a fort. They could also be constructed even further away from the fort and its outer works.[25] No matter where a redoubt was built, however, the main purpose was always clear: redoubts could serve as a first line of defense in the face of enemy fire or invasion. There was not any uniform way in which to build redoubts, and therefore, they tended to be of various shapes, constructions and appearances. According to historian Brian Leigh Dunnigan, redoubts were "any small, self-contained fortification without flanking devices such as bastions…from small, square, round or polygonal forts to the familiar log blockhouse of the American frontier when the latter stood alone and was not part of a larger fort."[26] The Fort Pitt Block House—and presumably the other redoubts of Fort Pitt—was different from more traditional redoubts in that it had a roof, therefore making it seem more like a blockhouse.

This begs the question: what is a blockhouse? The term *blockhouse* is most likely derived from the German word *blochaus*, which means "a house which blocks a pass."[27] Blockhouses were almost entirely an American innovation as they were mainly used on the frontier as a way to defend European settlers from American Indian attacks. While blockhouses were commonly stand-alone structures used by settlers for defense and/or shelter, they could also be found as part of larger fortifications. Similar to redoubts, blockhouses could take many different shapes and be constructed out of many different materials. To use the words of Dunnigan once again, "a blockhouse was not necessarily a redoubt, [but] it could serve the purposes of one."[28] While it is no question that the Fort Pitt Block House was originally built as a redoubt for Fort Pitt, its appearance was so similar to a traditional blockhouse that it had become officially named as such by the end of the nineteenth century.

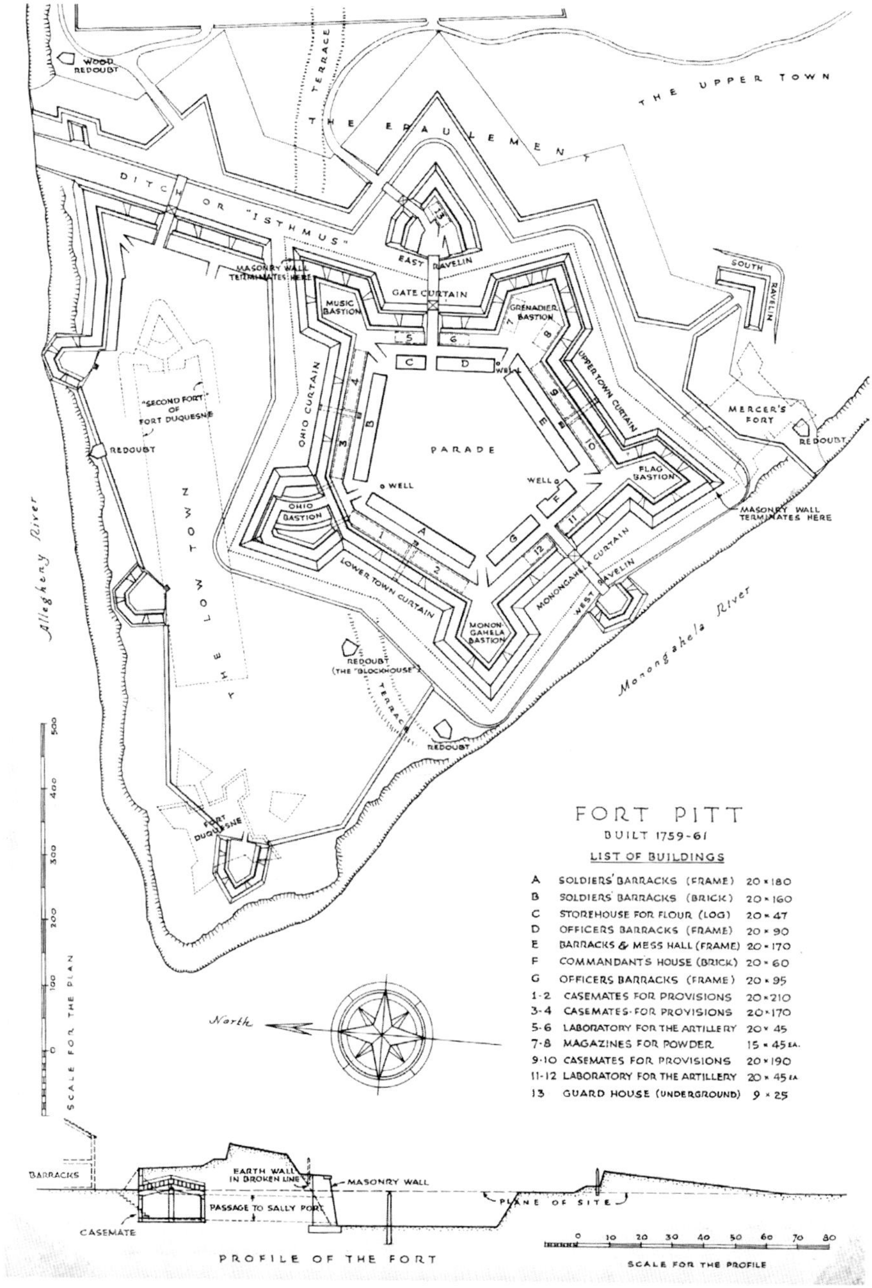

A plan of Fort Pitt by Charles M. Stotz. The plan not only shows the fort but also depicts the placement of the redoubts or blockhouses around the exterior of the fort. Faint outlines of the location Fort Duquesne and Mercer's Fort are also visible. *Courtesy of the Thomas & Katherine Detre Library and Archives, Sen. John Heinz History Center.*

Unfortunately, it is not as clear as to whether or not the Block House was one of the two built by December 1763 or if it was the third redoubt built presumably no later than February 1764 (as seen in Bouquet's quote earlier). It is known that by the fall of 1764, five redoubts, including the Block House, surrounded the outer walls of Fort Pitt. There were two redoubts along the side of the fort facing the Monongahela River, with one around the area of the Flag Bastion and the other next to the Monongahela Bastion. There were two more redoubts along the Allegheny River side of Fort Pitt, one located near the Ohio/Lower Bastion and the other closer to the Music Bastion.[29] The Block House was built in front of the fort facing toward the tip of the Point, directly in between the Ohio and Monongahela Bastions. The building still remains in this location today, having never been moved or relocated.

It is generally assumed that all of the redoubts were of similar construction to the Block House (brick and stone), with the exception of the fifth redoubt near the Music Bastion, which was built entirely out of wood. In a letter to Bouquet from May 15, 1764, Captain William Grant stated that "we are Just now finishing an Oven at the Redoubt in the upper Town Sufficiently large for the troops against their arrival. [T]he repairs of the Post are quite done, and the Wooden Redoubt is well picqueted."[30] The other redoubt referred to in the "upper town" was known as Grant's Redoubt, a large defensive structure built around February 1764. Still standing in Pittsburgh at the foot of Redoubt Alley in the early nineteenth century, it was eventually torn down sometime before the 1850s, presumably to make way for more housing and businesses.[31]

The Original Construction of the Block House

The Block House itself was originally built as a two-story, five-sided structure. The back wall and two sidewalls were built at right angles to each other, with the two front walls forming a point or triangle. The point of the Block House faces northwest toward the area where the Ohio River begins, and the back wall faces to the southeast.[32] The structure is 23 feet wide and 26 feet deep overall. The sidewalls measure 16 feet long, with the walls forming the building's point each measuring at 15 feet. The base of the building covers 483 square feet.[33] The overall construction of the Block House consists of a stone foundation followed by a wooden course line of gun loops. Resting on

Soldier reenactors demonstrating how the firing step and gun loopholes would have been used in the Block House. *Photo by Roy Engelbrecht.*

the top of these gun loops is a brick wall, and on the top of the brick wall runs another course line of wooden gun loops. A shorter brick wall follows next with the wooden rafters and roof capping off the entire structure.

As previously stated, the purpose of the Block House and other redoubts was to provide additional defense for the entire fortification, particularly those sections most damaged by the previous floods. Soldiers were stationed in the redoubts throughout the day and the night, working in shifts to keep watch over the fort. Since both floors of the Block House had a set of gun loops running along the entire course of the building, the soldiers could utilize both floors as lookouts for possible attacks. If an enemy did try to attack, the soldiers in the redoubts could fire their muskets through the gun loops. In the lower floor of the Block House, the gun loops were purposely built above the heads of the soldiers, whose average height was around five feet, five inches.[34] By using a firing step encircling the room, the soldiers could step up, look out and/or fire their weapons and step back down within the safety of the stone foundation wall. Because there was less chance of enemy fire coming directly into the upstairs room, the gun loops there were built slightly above eye level—the level appropriate for firing a gun. This means that the soldiers in the upper floor stood directly on the wooden floor, further confirming their average height.

The base or foundation of the Block House was constructed of both natural and rough-cut limestone with a limestone-based mortar. The stone walls are about two feet thick and consist of two separate inner and outer layers joined together by header stones. Between these two layers was a filling made up of small stones and mixture of lime and sandy soil; this mixture is now more of a silt texture due to floodwaters over the years.[35] When the Block House was built in 1764, the stone foundation walls stood well over seven feet above the ground on the exterior. Inside the structure, the lower floor consisted of wooden beams, with wooden planks placed across the beams. The height of the stone walls from the wooden floor to the first set of gun loops measured close to seven feet, making it necessary for the soldiers to have the firing step mentioned previously.[36] During the nineteenth century, when the Point became a residential and light industrial district, a lot of extra soil was brought in for flood-control and construction purposes. Although much of this was eventually removed during the building of Point State Park, there is still much more ground surrounding the Block House than there would have been originally in 1764. As a result, the stone walls stand today at roughly four feet above ground level on the exterior. Inside the Block House, the walls stand at five feet, four inches, with sixteen inches below the outer ground level.[37]

The wooden gun loops that encircled the Block House both upstairs and downstairs were made entirely out of white oak, each set being hand-hewn. As mentioned, these gun loops or loopholes were the holes through which soldiers could look out for enemies, as well as where they could fire their weapons. Loopholes had been in place since the Middle Ages in Europe, where they originally used for firing arrows from castle walls and other fortresses.[38] Being an eighteenth-century defensive structure, the Block House's loopholes were built specifically for musket fire, with no cannons or larger artillery used in the structure. Each opening was cut at a different angle so as to provide the best defense possible. On the interior, the openings were wide and tall to allow for a better range of motion with the soldiers' muskets, but they tapered downward so that the exterior openings were narrower and much smaller. This made it very difficult for enemy fire to enter the building. There were originally twenty-two openings in each set of gun loops, including ten smaller openings at each corner of the building both upstairs and downstairs. Because of changes to the Block House over time, some of these openings have been obliterated by restoration and repair or, in the case of one loophole, by a new doorway. Despite these changes, 60 percent of the gun loops in the Block House are original from 1764, making them a special and important feature to the structure today.[39]

The original entrance to the Block House was located on the south sidewall in its lower left corner. By examining a painting of the Block House from 1832, it can be seen that a door was placed in that corner underneath the first set of gun loops, with the gun loops almost serving as a lintel for the door.[40] Because the 1832 painting is the earliest known original image of the Block House, and since it shows no other openings, it can be reasonably assumed that the door featured in the painting was, in fact, the same door used by the soldiers in 1764. It is also important to note that by placing the door underneath the gun loops, the defensive course line around the lower floor was not interrupted like it is by the modern entrance door to the building.

CHANGES FOR FORT PITT AND THE BLOCK HOUSE

The Fort Pitt Block House continued to be used as a military structure for the next eight years, as Fort Pitt remained an active British fort. The people who lived around the fort depended on its garrison for defense from possible Native American attacks. The British Royal Proclamation of 1763, signed in October, essentially set aside lands west of the Appalachian Mountains strictly for use by the Indians. No white settlement was permitted beyond the proclamation's boundary line, and any white settlers already living on the land were ordered to leave.[41]

Despite these restrictions, white settlement continued at a rate alarming to both the Indians and the British government. As chaos intensified on the frontier, the British government realized that further steps had to be taken. One step was the Treaty of Fort Stanwix in November 1768, which created a new boundary line farther west starting from Fort Stanwix along the Mohawk River in New York, going down to the south and the west where the Ohio River meets the Kanawha River and following the Ohio out to its confluence with the Tennessee River.[42] In exchange for ceding more land, the Indian delegation received more than £10,000; however, the Indians who signed the treaty were the Iroquois nations, acting on behalf of the Ohio Indians. Tribes such as the Shawnees, Delawares and Mingos still resided in the new territory ceded to Britain. This meant that when white settlement began to push into the area, conflict continued since the Ohio Indians felt the land rightly belonged to them.[43]

Following the Treaty of Fort Stanwix, the British government took yet another step in attempting to end the fighting on the frontier. This step was the decommissioning of some of its westerns posts and forts, including Fort Pitt. By closing these forts, the British hoped to appease the Indians while at the same time reduce the heavy spending going into the upkeep of the western posts. The French and Indian War had been costly for the British government, and forts such as Fort Pitt were a drain on already low funds. By the fall of 1772, the garrison of Fort Pitt had officially been given word from General Gage that it was to begin the abandonment of the fort as soon as possible. While leaving Fort Pitt seemed plausible to the British government, it was not acceptable to the settlers living around the fort. Reverend David McClure, a missionary who was visiting Fort Pitt at the time of Gage's announcement, had this to say:

> *In consequence of orders from General Gage, the garrison are preparing to depart. They have begun to destroy the fortress. This is a matter of surprise & grief to the people around, who have requested that the fortress may stand, as a place of security to them, in case in* [I]*ndian invasion. I asked one of the officers, the reason of their destroying a Fort, so necessary to the safety of the frontiers? He replied, "The Americans will not submit to the* [B]*ritish Parliament, and they may now defend themselves."*[44]

Almost immediately, the people of Pittsburgh began to petition the governor of Pennsylvania, insisting that they needed protection from American Indian attacks. The governor took up their cause and requested that the Pennsylvania Assembly consider keeping an active garrison at Fort Pitt. In February 1773, the governor and the settlers received a reply from the Assembly:

> [W]*e are led to conclude that the uneasiness of the Back Settlers is without Foundation, and by no means a sufficient Reason for a Measure which we fear may be productive of the very mischiefs it may be intended to avert*... [O]*n the Contrary, the maintaining of Garrisons in or near* [the Indians'] *Country, has been frequently an object of their Jealousy and Complaints...that Measure* [of evacuating Fort Pitt] *is so entirely agreeable to them, that it is likely to effect a Removal of their Jealousies, and a Conciliation of their Affections to this Province.*"[45]

Seeing no reason to keep the garrison and hoping to maintain peace with the Indians, the Pennsylvania Assembly dismissed Pittsburgh's complaints. This reply, whether good or bad, may not have mattered anyway because the fort had already been sold to private citizens by its commander, Captain Charles Edmonstone. In fact, he had sold the fort and its earthworks on October 10, 1772, close to the time he received official word to abandon the garrison. The private citizens were business partners William Thompson and Alexander Ross, and they purchased the entire Fort Pitt for fifty pounds in New York currency. The sale included all of the bricks, stone, ironwork and wood making up the fort and its buildings. The bill of sale specifically mentioned the inclusion of two redoubts, presumably two of the five redoubts surrounding Fort Pitt.[46]

Was the Block House one of these two redoubts? It is likely that it was since one of Alexander Ross's other business partners, Alexander McKee, had been using the structure to conduct trade with the Indians. McKee was well known throughout the Ohio Territory as an agent for the British Indian Department, a fur trader and a land speculator. Born of a white father and an Indian mother, McKee began his service in Indian affairs as an assistant for Deputy Indian Agent George Croghan in the 1750s. By the early 1770s, he had acquired 1,400 acres of land along the Ohio River below Fort Pitt (modern-day McKees Rocks), beginning his interests in land speculation in the West. His work as a fur trader among the Indians began around the same time, leading to his partnership with Alexander Ross.[47]

A late nineteenth-century rendition of how the Block House may have looked in 1764. Images such as these may have influenced how the Block House was restored later in 1894. *From* A History of the Catholic Church in the Dioceses of Pittsburg and Allegheny *(1880)*.

According to letters written between General Gage and McKee in September 1772, McKee had requested his personal use of a "small brick outbuilding" located outside Fort Pitt's main walls. Since Gage and Edmonstone were in the process of decommissioning the fort and no longer needed the structure, they saved it for McKee's use.[48] This evidence, coupled with the knowledge that McKee's partner, Alexander Ross, purchased the fort along with two of its redoubts by October 1772, further points to the possibility that the Block House was used by McKee. More than 230 years later, in 2003, an archaeological excavation of the floor of the Block House uncovered, among other specimens, a considerable amount of various types of ammunition. This amount suggests that the Block House may have been used for other purposes such as a trading post or a storehouse for munitions. A large number of glass beads and wampum beads used in trading on the frontier were also discovered in the excavation.[49] Knowing that Alexander McKee was operating a trading facility out of a small brick outbuilding at Fort Pitt and knowing that Pittsburgh itself was a major point of trade in the Ohio River Valley, it is very likely that the Block House was used as a trading post.

Around the time that the Block House became a trading post, Fort Pitt became the center stage of a decades-long conflict between the colonies of Virginia and Pennsylvania. Before the French and Indian War, Pennsylvania and Virginia argued over which colony had jurisdiction over the Forks of the Ohio. During the war, the fighting briefly subsided only to escalate even further following the war's end. Pennsylvania believed that Pittsburgh and its surrounding areas belonged under its domain since the region was directly west of its eastern settlements and since many Pennsylvanians had already begun to live there. Virginia felt very strongly that Fort Pitt belonged to its western districts, and there were quite a number of Pittsburgh residents who considered themselves Virginians. Virginia also felt that it had physically earned the right to control the Pittsburgh region since it was the Virginia militia that fought bravely throughout the French and Indian War to protect the area for British interests. When Pennsylvania formed Westmoreland County in February 1773, it placed Pittsburgh under the county's jurisdiction. This angered the governor of Virginia, John Murray, Earl of Dunmore, who decided to take control of Fort Pitt by force in January 1774.[50]

When Lord Dunmore took over Fort Pitt, the fort was under the command of Major Edward Ward, who supposedly had been given permission by Ross and Thompson to maintain a small garrison at the site. Removing Ward from his post, Dunmore proceeded to place Dr. John Connolly, an ambitious Pennsylvanian, in charge of the fort. Although Connolly was arrested by authorities from Westmoreland County shortly after he came to Pittsburgh, he managed to escape just before his trial. Returning by March 1774, Connolly officially announced Pittsburgh as part of the West Augusta District of Virginia and took over the fort with a group of militia. He renamed the garrison Fort Dunmore in honor of his superior.[51] These events began what is known as Dunmore's War, a brief conflict that lasted for a little over a year.

BEGINNING OF THE END

Dunmore's War was quickly overshadowed by the onset of the American Revolution. The events of Lexington and Concord in Massachusetts in April 1775 occurred simultaneously with the ongoing struggles at Fort Dunmore/Pitt. By June, Lord Dunmore had fled Virginia, escaping to Britain with his family. Dr. Connolly followed soon thereafter, and with no one left to uphold the fight, Dunmore's War came to an abrupt end. Virginia, now under the control of a Patriot assembly, replaced Connolly with Captain John Neville as commandant of Fort Pitt (back under its original name). Neville remained until February 1777, when he was relieved by Captain Robert Campbell. Brigadier General Edward Hand arrived in June 1777, formally taking command of Fort Pitt on behalf of the Continental army.[52] It was during Hand's command that Fort Pitt became the western headquarters for the Continental army, a role it held for the rest of the war.

It can be assumed that during this time the Block House remained a trading post since Alexander McKee remained active in the Pittsburgh area. This was the Revolution, however, and many Pittsburgh residents joined with the Patriots' cause, while others remained on the side of the Loyalists, faithful to the Crown. Although never fully confirming where his loyalties lay, McKee was known for his strong ties to the British government as a member of the Indian Department, as well as for his connections to the Ohio Indian tribes. People feared his ability to steer the ever-threatening Indians over to the British side. This fear finally came to the attention of Hand, who ordered McKee to report to eastern Pennsylvania on suspicion of Loyalist activities. Afraid for his life, McKee escaped from Pittsburgh in March 1778 along with other Loyalists from the region.[53]

It is unknown if the Block House remained in use as a trading post following McKee's departure. In fact, the entire period between 1778 and 1785 is a very hazy one for the Block House as barely anything survives to explain what the building could have been used for during that time. Since there was a major war and Fort Pitt was once again an active garrison, it is possible that the Block House briefly returned to its original purpose as a defensive structure. It is also possible that someone else maintained it as a trading site or storage facility. Perhaps it simply stood vacant for a number of years. Some evidence is provided in a letter written by Fort Pitt's newest commandant, Colonel Daniel Brodhead, in June 1779:

> *The inhabitants of this place are continually encroaching on what I conceive to be the rights of the Garrison and which was always considered as such when the Fort was occupied by the King of Britain's Troops. They have now the assurance to erect their fences within a few yards of the Bastion... The Block-houses likewise which are part of the strength of the place are occupied and claimed by private persons to the injury of the service.*[54]

Not too specific, but the point is clear: the Block House and the other redoubts were no longer in active military use by the summer of 1779. Whether Brodhead was successful in removing these "private persons" from the redoubts is not known. More important issues were at hand for the colonel as the Revolution continued on the frontier. The next major change for both Fort Pitt and the Block House would come soon enough as the new decade approached.

Chapter 2

Living in the Block House

[A] *small brick house, with arched windows and doorways, now inhabited by the "lowest class"*…

By the 1780s, Fort Pitt and the Block House were entering into new yet different stages in their histories. The end of the eighteenth century would see the ending of Fort Pitt but the beginning of the Block House in its new role as a residential structure. Numerous families of different classes and backgrounds occupied the building for more than one hundred years, transforming the Block House into one of the countless tenements in the Point District of Pittsburgh. Because people were using the building as a home and not a defensive redoubt, the Block House had several changes made to its structure, including the addition of windows, multiple door openings and a fireplace. Despite these changes, it is important to remember that if the Block House had not been used as a residence for such a long time, it would not be standing today. These families—whether they realized it or not—saved the Block House from ultimate destruction during an era when historic preservation was more or less nonexistent.

The Selling of the Point

The American Revolution ended in 1783 with the signing of the Treaty of Paris. The United States Army, now in permanent control of Fort Pitt, decided to maintain a small garrison in Pittsburgh due to continued threats of Indian attacks. The lands on which the fort and the town of Pittsburgh stood were owned by the Penn family. William Penn, the founder of the colony of Pennsylvania, had long since passed away, but his sons and grandsons still remained as powerful proprietors. In November 1779, the Pennsylvania Assembly ordered all lands belonging to the Penn family that were surveyed and returned to the Land Office after July 1776 to be forfeited to the Commonwealth. The land in which Pittsburgh was situated had been surveyed and sent to the Land Office in 1769, so it remained under the ownership of the Penn family.[55] By the end of the Revolution, however, the family had begun to sell some of its property, including the Pittsburgh holdings.

The first people to purchase property from the Penn family in Pittsburgh were Major Isaac Craig and his business partner, Lieutenant Colonel Stephen Bayard. Both men had served as officers at Fort Pitt during the Revolution. Bayard and Craig realized the potential that Pittsburgh had to offer in land and business opportunities. Following the end of the war, the two men formed a business partnership simply called Craig, Bayard & Company. They were interested in such ventures as whiskey production and moving goods across the frontier, but land speculation was the key to their plans for success. On January 22, 1784, Craig and Bayard made an agreement with the Penn family to purchase the Point. The actual deed for the property was not signed until December 31 of that year due to the town of Pittsburgh being surveyed by the Penn family. The final purchase was made up of thirty-two lots of property between West Street and Marbury Street, including the land on which Fort Pitt stood.[56]

Six months following the purchase agreement in January 1784, Craig and Bayard formed a new partnership with William Turnbull, Pierre Marmie and John Holker of Philadelphia. Turnbull, Marmie and Holker already operated an established firm with similar goals to Craig, Bayard & Company. They had plans to construct a sawmill near Pittsburgh, as well as a whiskey distillery and an iron furnace, but above all, they were interested in real estate. They especially looked to Craig and Bayard, both being from the Pittsburgh region, for assistance in this matter. As stated previously, the actual deed for the Point property was not signed until December 31, 1784. According to the deed, the property was sold only to Craig and Bayard; however, days later on January 4, 1785, the Point was changed over to a gentleman named Daniel Britt (most likely an agent), who in turn sold it back to Turnbull, Marmie & Company the following day. Now the property was in the hands of all five businessmen, not just Craig and Bayard.[57]

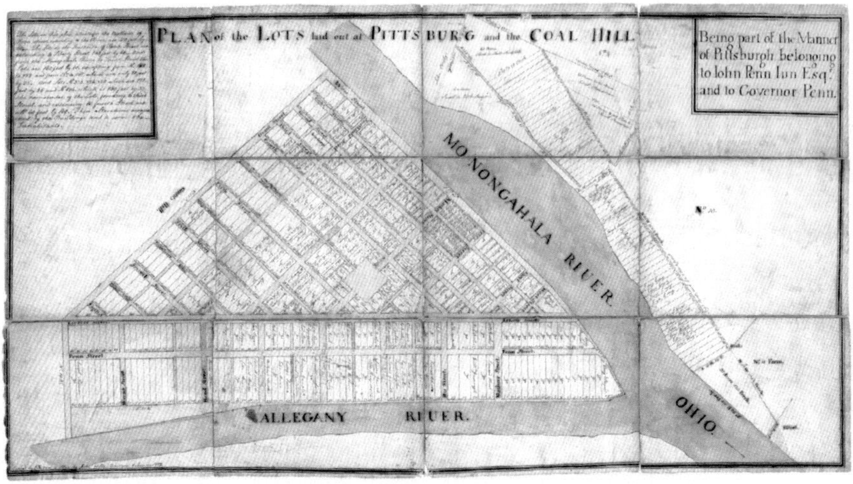

A 1787 map and plan of the lots laid out in Pittsburgh following the sale of the Penn property. The entire Point, bounded by Marbury Street and West Street, belonged to Craig & Bayard. *Darlington Digital Library Maps, courtesy of the Archives Service Center, University of Pittsburgh.*

ISAAC CRAIG MOVES INTO THE BLOCK HOUSE

It was most likely after the final deed purchase in January 1785 that Isaac Craig and his family moved into the Block House. According to his son, Neville Craig, the firm of Turnbull, Marmie & Company built an addition next to the Block House, "thus constituting a dwelling house."[58] Neville Craig also claimed that William Turnbull lived in the new house for a year, with Isaac Craig moving in by 1786. If Neville Craig's statement is true, then Turnbull would be considered the first official resident of the Block House; however, nothing has ever been found to back this claim. It has also been discovered through recent research that Neville Craig tended to embellish the facts when it came to his father, leaving his authenticity as questionable.[59]

The claim that Isaac Craig and his family occupied the Block House and adjoining structure from circa 1785 to 1789 is true, however, and Craig is recognized as the first person to live in the Block House. He was also the wealthiest person to ever live in the Block House, as by 1785 he was quite well-to-do. Born in Ireland in 1742, Craig immigrated to Philadelphia in 1768 with the intention of becoming a carpenter. His military career began during the American Revolution in 1775 when he joined the Continental army as a lieutenant captain in the Marine Corps. He continued to serve in various capacities, earning a captain's commission in the army in 1776. He was briefly sent to Fort Pitt in the summer of 1779 to serve under Colonel John Proctor and General Edward Hand. Spending winter quarters in Carlisle, Pennsylvania, he returned to Fort Pitt in June 1780. It was there that he met Lieutenant Colonel Stephen Bayard, who was second in command at the fort. By the end of the war, he had become "Major" Isaac Craig, and he began to move into business ventures.[60]

Neville B. Craig, the oldest son of Major Isaac Craig. Neville was born in 1787, when the Craig family occupied the Block House. *From* Colonial and Revolutionary Families of Pennsylvania, *vol. 2 (1911).*

Why would Isaac Craig want to live in the Block House? At the time of moving into the redoubt, Craig probably had two issues to consider. First, while he was busy with land transactions and forming companies, he managed to find time to marry one of the most eligible women in Pittsburgh. Her name was Amelia Neville, only daughter of the wealthy and respected General John Neville.[61] Now that he was married and on the way toward starting a family, Craig had to find a suitable place to live. The Block House was probably viewed as a nice, sturdy structure that could easily be converted into a dwelling or part of a dwelling. The Craig family most likely used the larger addition as their actual dwelling, with the Block House as an annex or outdoor kitchen. It also would have been important to Craig to be close to where his company's projects were taking place. Not only was the Block House located directly at the heart of the Point (the firm's newest property holding), but it was also near the locations of where they planned to build the whiskey distillery and the sawmill.

It might be odd to think of a family living in proximity to an active fort. Although the ground underneath Fort Pitt was now privately owned, the fort itself was still occupied by the United States Army, with the government paying Turnbull & Company for use of the fort. That being said, there were only about four to twelve men garrisoned at Fort Pitt during this time, and despite continued threats from Native American Indians on the frontier, the fort did not see any military action following the American Revolution.[62] The Craig family would not have been in any immediate danger while living in the Block House.

The Point Switches Hands

Isaac Craig occupied the Block House and adjoining structure for about four years, from 1785 to 1789. During that time, Craig's eldest son, Neville, was born in 1787. The following year, Craig became one of the original petitioners for the creation of Allegheny County. While Craig was building a family and becoming more prominent in his community, his business ventures began to take a turn for the worse. His partnership with Turnbull & Company was starting to crumble. Stephen Bayard had actually left the partnership by 1788, going on to eventually found Elizabeth Township just south of Pittsburgh. When the company's military contracts failed to bring in revenue, Turnbull and Marmie placed most of the blame on Craig.[63]

It is unclear as to why Craig ultimately decided to move out of the Block House, although his failing partnership with Turnbull may have had a hand in it. Craig and his family initially moved into Bower Hill, the mansion of Amelia Craig's father, John Neville. The family later moved to Water Street in Pittsburgh (not far from the Point) but ultimately settled on Neville Island on the Ohio River.[64]

By the summer of 1791, Isaac Craig was facing lawsuits brought against him by his fellow business partners. At the same time, he was appointed deputy quartermaster general for the United States Army, serving this position at Fort Pitt.[65] The fort's days were coming to an end, however, and Craig was placed in charge of building a new garrison farther upstream along the Allegheny River. This small fort, completed in May 1792, was named Fort Lafayette (or "Fort Fayette," as it was commonly known). Before and during the construction of Fort Fayette, Fort Pitt was torn down and sold off by Turnbull & Company.[66]

Despite the ongoing lawsuits, the Point remained under the ownership of Turnbull, Marmie, Holker and Craig until 1795, when Craig was legally forced to sign over his share of the property.[67] Turnbull & Company continued to own the property until February 1797, when it sold the deed to Peter Shiras and Robert Smith. Peter Shiras was originally from Mount Holly, New Jersey, where he was an established member of the community. In 1794, his eldest son, George Shiras, was sent to western Pennsylvania with the New Jersey militia to quash the Whiskey Rebellion. While on this campaign, George spent a considerable amount of time in Pittsburgh. Realizing the opportunities to be had in this frontier town, George convinced his father to move the family to Pittsburgh in the summer of 1795.[68]

Rare image of Peter Shiras, the owner of the Point District and the Block House from 1797 to 1802. Shiras and his family owned and operated the Point Brewery. *From* Justice George Shiras, Jr., of Pittsburgh *(1953).*

It is generally claimed that Peter Shiras and Robert Smith (presumably a business partner about whom little is known) began operating a brewery at the Point in 1795 called "Point Brewery." This seems to be based solely on a brief newspaper article in the *Pittsburgh Gazette* dated November 14, 1795, announcing the opening of the brewery.[69] Although Shiras and Smith may have begun operations as early as November 1795, it is clear from the deed that they did not officially own the property of the Point until 1797. By June of that year, Robert Smith had sold his interest in the property to Peter Shiras, leaving Shiras as the sole proprietor of the brewery and the Point.[70]

Peter Shiras and his family presumably lived at the Point in proximity to their brewery, for according to genealogist and historian John W. Jordan, Peter's son, George, built "a house out of bricks from the old magazine" of Fort Pitt.[71] Shiras's great-great-grandson, George Shiras III, recalled it as being "unclear" as to where the family lived at the Point, although he believed that they may have occupied one of the old barracks buildings left behind from the fort.[72] There is no mention of the family living in the Block House, but it is hard to believe that the structure did not play some part since it was directly across from the brewery structure. Shiras continued to own the Point and operate the brewery for the next five years. In 1802, he decided to retire back to New Jersey and sell his share of the Point, including the brewery. Selling his property back to Robert Smith, Peter Shiras left Pittsburgh in the autumn of 1802, never to return. His three sons, including George, stayed behind. George Shiras continued on as manager of the brewery.

THE O'HARA YEARS

Although he was now the owner of the Point, Robert Smith was most likely acting as an agent on behalf of another gentleman, James O'Hara.[73] James O'Hara was a well-known and respected figure throughout the Pittsburgh area. Born in Ireland in about 1752, O'Hara immigrated to America when he was twenty years old and found work as a trader with the Indians in the West. He joined the Continental army at the start of the American Revolution, becoming a captain and serving as an assistant quartermaster throughout the war. In 1783, he married a well-to-do woman named Mary Carson and settled in Pittsburgh. It was after moving to Pittsburgh that O'Hara began his careers in business and real estate, while continuing to serve the military in various capacities, including quartermaster general for the United States Army (his deputy was none other than Isaac Craig). He purchased large tracts of land throughout Pittsburgh during this time, and along with Craig, he opened one of the first glass factories west of the Allegheny Mountains in 1797.[74] This factory was located directly across from the Point on the south side of the Monongahela River. The glass bottles manufactured by O'Hara and Craig were used by

An early twentieth-century rendition of James O'Hara as he may have looked in his younger days. *Courtesy of the Fort Pitt Society Collections.*

none other than the Point Brewery, for O'Hara had been operating the site since 1803.[75]

O'Hara had originally formed a partnership with a master brewer from Europe named Joseph Coppinger in about 1802. Together they continued the brewery that Peter Shiras had started. Coppinger eventually left the brewery, however, with George Shiras returning as manager.[76] An excellent description of both the Point and the Block House during this time is provided by a young man named John Fanning Watson. Watson had also formed a partnership with O'Hara involving the shipping of goods to New Orleans. Visiting the Point in 1804, Watson had this to say:

> *A part of the brew-house premises fills the place which was a bastion* [of the fort]*; at a little distance from it is still there, a small brick five-sided edifice, called the guard-house, erected by the British…It has two ranges of loop holes through sticks of timber, let into the walls, which are a foot thick. In one of its sides, near the top, is a relic, a tablet of stone…on which is inscribed "A.D. 1764, Col. Bouquet." Adjoining to this guard-house are*

One of the earliest depictions of Pittsburgh, painted in about 1804 by George Beck. The viewpoint is taken from farther down the Ohio River, looking back at the Point, with the town of Pittsburgh rising behind it. *Courtesy of the University Library System, University of Pittsburgh.*

> *now two small brick houses, which were built from the walls of Fort Pitt. I saw these things in 1804. Then the area of the fort, excepting the said brew-house premises, of Shiras, was all a nearly levelled* [sic] *grass field, from General O'Hara's residence, where I dwelt, down to the point.*[77]

This description is very interesting not only because it is one of the earliest descriptions of the Block House but also because of the amount of information Watson provides in a single paragraph. The "two small brick houses" adjoining the Block House were most likely the structures built previously by Isaac Craig. Watson also mentions that they were made of Fort Pitt bricks (which would prove important later in Block House history).

The one aspect that Watson does not mention is who—if anyone—was occupying the Block House during this time, although he does indicate that there were very few other structures at the Point aside from the brewery and the Block House. The time period between 1789 and 1836 is, in fact, a murky one for the Block House. It has generally been assumed that it continued to be used as a residence following Craig's departure, but there is nothing to prove this assumption. Large amounts of glass fragments collected during an archaeological dig of the floor inside the Block House seem to suggest other possible uses for the building.[78] One theory for the excess of glass is that the Point Brewery used the redoubt to store its empty glass bottles. These would be the same glass bottles made at O'Hara's glass factory across the river. If the Block House was a storage facility for the brewery, it is still unknown how long it would have been used for such purposes.

THE BLOCK HOUSE BECOMES A TENEMENT

Robert Smith continued to own the Point until September 1805, when it was purchased outright by James O'Hara.[79] O'Hara lived on for another fourteen years until his death in 1819. Leaving behind a vast amount of land, his Point property was inherited by his second daughter, Mary O'Hara Croghan. Mary and her husband, William Croghan, were now the official owners of the Point. Mary did not live long, passing away in 1827 after the birth of her second child. This child also died shortly thereafter, leaving behind Mary's grieving husband and their one-year-old daughter, Mary Elizabeth.[80] Under the guardianship of her father and a group of trustees, young Mary Elizabeth was the new owner of the Point. All of the

A portrait of Mary Elizabeth Croghan Schenley at the time of her marriage to Captain Edward W.H. Schenley in 1842. *Courtesy of the Fort Pitt Society Collections.*

leasing revenue collected from the inhabitants and businesses of the Point would go directly into her coffers.

The Shiras family continued to operate the brewery on behalf of O'Hara and his heirs until at least 1835, when Shiras moved the brewery closer to the center of town.[81] Around this time, the Point became much more populated as other families and businesses began to lease the land from the O'Hara estate. When John Fanning Watson returned to the Point in 1834, he remarked that the district was "now filled with dwellings."[82] Initially, the Point (and the Block House) was inhabited by people of many different social classes.

The first official "interview" with a Block House inhabitant took place in 1836 by a travel writer named W.G. Lyford. Lyford, collecting information for his new travel book, *The Western Address Directory*, arrived in Pittsburgh in December 1836. Intrigued by the city's French and Indian War history, he ventured down to the Point to see the former sites of Fort Pitt and Fort Duquesne. Upon finding the Block House, he noticed the same exact stone tablet on the building's southern wall that Watson saw years before, reading "A.D. 1764 ~ Coll. Bouquet." Lyford stated that he asked the occupant, a German man named John Martin, if he could enter the building. Martin obliged, and Lyford began asking him questions about the history of the structure. Although Lyford found the first floor of the Block House to be "tastefully finished and furnished," Martin could provide him with little information aside from his monthly rent of forty dollars. When Lyford suggested that Martin open the building for tours and offer lemonade and other treats to visitors, "his wife just at this moment entered the room, laughing, from an adjoining shed, and wiping her arms (for she appeared to have been washing,) 'dare Jon, didn't I dell de so, ofden? hear vat de man say!' John laughed likewise, and replied 'ah, I'ms doo old now; and presides, yoo nose I cot vorkpetterdan dat.'"[83]

Lyford finished his brief account by mentioning that the Block House was difficult to find, being surrounded by lumberyards and workshops. Because of Lyford's historic visit, it can be stated for certain that by 1836 the Block House was a single-family residence located in the heart of a bustling neighborhood in a growing city. It had an "adjoining shed," as evidenced by the appearance of John Martin's wife, and its lower floor was "tastefully furnished." Lyford's account makes clear that the Martins were of a middle class in which they could afford a forty-dollar monthly rent and tastefully finished rooms, but they were also laborers without the help of servants. Finally, for John Martin's wife to have made such a comment indicates that the Block House often received visitors interested in its history and connection to Fort Pitt. Although the Martins could not provide such a history, they clearly understood the significance of the building they called home.

As the Point District became more residential, descriptions and drawings of its streets were provided in city directories and maps. One directory actually provided information on how to locate the Block House in the Point. In his 1850 directory for Pittsburgh, Samuel Fahnestock remarked that "the Redoubt" was located between Point Street and Point Alley. To access the Block House site, a person would have to walk from Point Street toward the Monongahela River along a nine-foot-wide alley named Brewery Alley. Forty-six feet from Point Street, the Block House could be viewed eight feet north of the alley. Fahnestock briefly mentioned the former Isaac Craig House, referring to it as "the back portion" of the Block House, being built by Turnbull, Marmie & Company in 1785. Fahnestock ended his description with this remark: "It is greatly to be desired, that [the Redoubt] should be preserved and kept in repair."[84]

WHY WOULD SOMEONE LIVE HERE?

Perhaps one of the most often-asked questions concerning the inhabitants of the Block House is why anyone would want to live in such a tiny building. As mentioned previously, Isaac Craig chose to live there due to its proximity to the landholdings and business ventures of Turnbull, Marmie & Company. But what of the others? Why would a person such as John Martin want to live in the Block House? It is important to remember that by the beginning of the nineteenth century, the Point District had become just another part of the town's residential and business areas. It was no longer the site of a fort, and it was no longer being used militarily. The purchase of the Point by James O'Hara opened it up to new businesses, industries and housing. The Block House would have actually been a desirable structure, being made of stone and brick and already converted for residential use.

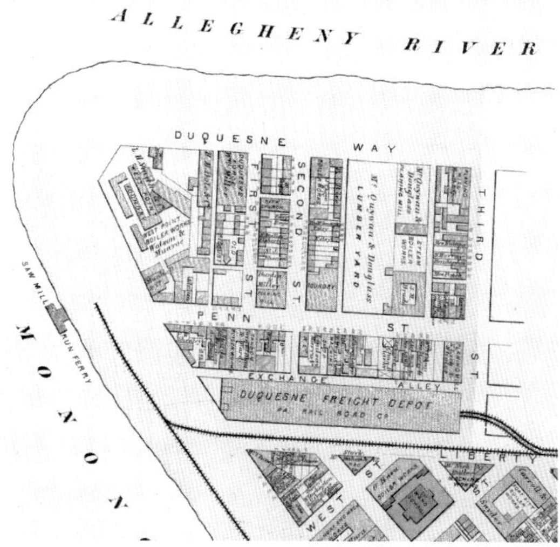

Map of the Point in 1872 showing the various housing, factories and mills throughout the district. The Block House and Isaac Craig House are marked along First Street (later renamed Fort Street) as "Old Redoubt." *Courtesy of G.M. Hopkins Maps Collections, Archives Service Center, University of Pittsburgh.*

During the early years, there were middle-class families, like Martin and his wife, living in the Block House and at the Point. This middle-class atmosphere quickly changed, however, as the neighborhood became more populated within the next decade. Waves of immigration flooded into Pittsburgh during the mid-nineteenth century, particularly from Ireland. Many of these Irish immigrants were impoverished and needed cheap housing close to their places of employment. The Point District, with its proximity to rivers prone to flooding and the ever-rising industry of the city, became less of a place for the middle and upper classes. Twenty years after Lyford's 1834 visit, another travel writer visiting the Point simply noted that the Block House was "a small brick house, with arched windows and doorways, now inhabited by the 'lowest class.'"[85]

As the Point changed into a crowded tenement district, more and more housing was needed. Homes that were previously used for single families were now divided into multi-family dwellings. The Block House was divided into a two-family residence as early as 1843.[86] One family occupied the first floor of the building; the other family lived on the second floor. According to historian Reverend A.A. Lambing, by 1880 the Point District had become "the most densely populated section of the city, and it would not be difficult

Street scene in the Point District, circa 1900. This may be a photograph of First Street, which was one block away from the Block House property. The slum conditions of the Point are visible in this image. *Courtesy of the Thomas & Katherine Detre Library and Archives, Sen. John Heinz History Center.*

to find at least one hundred families who occupy but a single room each, and that perhaps no more than twelve by fourteen feet. The people are, with very few exceptions, Irish Catholics…who settled here about twenty-five years ago, and the Irish language is spoken more generally here than in any other place out of their native isle."[87]

WHO LIVED HERE?

One of the most difficult aspects of the history of the Block House is learning who exactly lived in the structure and at what time. Although it may never be known how many families lived in the structure or the names of every family, sources have survived providing a view of what it was like to live in the Block House. Artwork, census results, city directories and brief written descriptions from newspapers and travel writers are provided throughout the mid- to late nineteenth century, along with a few firsthand accounts or interviews with actual inhabitants. All of these materials combined offer an interesting glimpse into the lives of these families, as well as the structural life of the Block House.

Writing in 1922, historian Charles Dahlinger claimed that a family by the name of McMahon occupied the Block House in the late 1850s and early 1860s, during which time a son was born named Michael J. McMahon. McMahon later became the principal of the Duquesne Public School located in the Point District. While records can be found showing that an "M.J. McMahon" served as principal of the Duquesne School in the late nineteenth/early twentieth centuries, there is nothing to back Dahlinger's claim that McMahon was born in the Block House.[88] Researching city directories from the time, however, does show that various McMahon families lived in the Point. In particular, there is a man named Owen McMahon who in 1863 is listed as living in the "upstairs" of 21 Point Alley. The Block House was located directly in between Point Alley and Point Street (later renamed First Street and then Fort Street), with its main entrances facing toward Point Alley. Could 21 Point Alley be the Block House? Was Owen McMahon related to Michael J. McMahon? Unfortunately, the full story of the McMahon family continues to be lost to history.[89]

There are other loose ends in the struggle to find Block House families. Two newspaper articles published in June 1914 mention the death of ninety-six-year-old Eliza Barnes. One article claims that Barnes was born in the Block House; the other notes that the Barnes family leased the entire Point and had been doing so since 1797.[90] This information strongly conflicts with the fact that the Point was owned entirely by Shiras and/or Smith from 1797 to 1805. While it is true that by the time of O'Hara everyone in the Point was leasing their properties, there is no trace of a Barnes family owning or leasing anything in the district. Another news article from 1935 announced the death of eighty-one-year-old Zephaniah B. Collins, "a lifelong resident of Pittsburgh who claimed the honor of being born in the old block house at the Point." This claim is actually more plausible because evidence can be found of the Collins family. The United States 1860 Census shows that six-year-old Zephaniah was living in Pittsburgh's First Ward (the Point) in 1860 with his family. The census does not clarify the street or the address; however, an 1859 city directory lists Zephaniah's father and eldest brother—both laborers—as living in

16 Point Alley. This could have been the Block House or a dwelling very close to the Block House.[91]

While nothing can be found to prove that the families listed here occupied the Block House, some evidence can be found for other families. One such family consisted of an Irish widow named Hannah Lee and her two young daughters, Mary and Margaret. The Lee family occupied the upper floor of the Block House from about 1877 to 1884. Much of what is known about them comes from a brief interview with Hannah Lee in 1880 and an extensive interview with her daughters in about 1943. The 1880 interview was conducted by a journalist from *Harper's New Monthly Magazine* as part of a larger article on the city of Pittsburgh. As part of his research for such an article, the journalist ventured down to the Point District for a glimpse of the last remaining structure of Fort Pitt. He found the Block House—with many of its gun loops still intact—and he also found Mrs. Lee, "a lady with a sunset tint in her hair and the quickness of temper that usually accompanies capillary ruddiness." Following a remark from the journalist on the building's quaintness, Mrs. Lee had this to say to her visitor:

> *If it's acquainted wid this house ye are, I wud be axin' yez for why I am payin' the sum of foive dollars the month's rint for the same, an' bud the two rooms of it, an the lady kapin' schtore on the flure below, an' payin' only the trifling sum of four dollars, an' she wid a big fine room.*[92]

This statement (while slightly amusing) provides much more information for historians today than it probably did for the *Harper's* journalist more than one hundred years ago. Based on this remark it can be determined that there were still two separate families occupying the Block House by 1880—the Lee family above and the "lady kapin' schtore" on the lower floor. It also provides a glimpse into the cost of living in the Block House. Mrs. Lee not only had to support herself and her two daughters—who at the time were ten and twelve years old—but she also had to pay their monthly rent of five dollars. This amount may seem incredibly small to us today, but considering the time (1880) and the place (one of the poorest neighborhoods in the city), five dollars probably consumed a significant portion of Lee's income. It is not known how Lee supported her family, although her occupation in the 1880 census is listed as "keeping house."[93]

Further information on Hannah Lee can be found in the 1943 interviews of her daughters by Wesley Bliss. Bliss conducted the interviews as part of his research for an archaeological dig of Fort Pitt. The Lee sisters were now

BLOCK-HOUSE OF FORT DUQUESNE.

An original sketch of the Block House from 1881. The person in the image is supposedly Hannah Lee, a woman who lived in the upper floor of the Block House from the late 1870s to the early 1880s. *From* Harper's Monthly Magazine *(1881).*

in their early seventies, but they provided a vast amount of information on their time in the Block House. They explained how their portion of the building was divided into two rooms by a partition. The partition was most likely nothing substantial or even permanent as there are no markings in the upstairs room today to indicate an actual wall was ever in place. Their claim of two rooms in the upstairs, however, was supported by their mother's remark more than sixty years earlier. The sisters also mentioned the Isaac Craig House, stating that it was a three-story house leased by a man named Martin Joyce, who in turn sublet it to various tenants. The women also mentioned that part of the Craig House was used as a saloon and that a family lived in its basement.[94]

Old Sibby Powers

The Lee sisters mentioned one other important piece of information that supported what their mother had stated years before them—that a woman lived below on the lower floor of the Block House, operating a candy store as a way to support herself. This leads into the story of Sibby Powers, one of the last inhabitants of the Fort Pitt Block House. Sibby Powers has gained a sort of fame today with Block House visitors since so much is known about her life while occupying the historic structure. Despite everything that is known about her, she still remains a mystery for reasons that will be explained.

The story of Sibby Powers begins in April 1894. The Block House had just been given to the Daughters of the American Revolution of Allegheny County, Pennsylvania (whose own story will be presented in the next chapter), and the society, wanting to restore the building back to its original appearance, began to evict the tenants from the Block House. The tenants at this time were an Irish widow named Sarah Costello living upstairs with her daughter, Delia, and another Irish widow named Sibby Powers living downstairs alone. The gifting of the Block House to the Daughters of the American Revolution made headlines, and newspaper reporters scrambled down to the Point to see the building and its inhabitants.

An interesting article from the *Pittsburgh Post* was published on April 23, 1894, in which Sibby Powers was interviewed about her time in the Block House. Much of what is known about Powers comes from this interview, particularly her candy store, which she used to help pay for her monthly rent of five dollars. Her "store" consisted of three shelves placed within a window that had been cut into the southern sidewall of the Block House. The window looked out toward Point Alley and the former Brewery Alley so that people passing by could see her store's display. Her wares included small cakes, stick candy, knives in a jar, "five dried-up ginger snaps," peppermint

One of the exhibits inside the Block House today is a replica of Sibby Powers's candy store. The exhibit is based on the *Pittsburgh Post* news article from 1894 in which Sibby's store was described in detail. *Photo by Roy Engelbrecht.*

drops, two spools of thread, a pack of hair pins, chewing gum and "two little oranges perched on two antiquated little teacups." The oranges were priced at two cents each. The reporter noted that aside from the window store, there were only boxes, a stove and an old bed in Sibby's portion of the Block House. Powers revealed in the interview that she had lived in the Block House for twenty-five years, having passed the age of sixty "long enough ago." If her memory is to be trusted, that would place her moving into the Block House in about 1869. She also stated that her husband had died thirty-five years ago, or about 1859.[95]

This interview would seem to tell it all—an Irish widow named Sibby Powers, living in a tenement for twenty-five years, paying five dollars monthly rent and operating a small store to support herself. But there are snags to this story. There are no references to anyone operating a store in the Block House until 1880, when Hannah Lee directly mentioned a store being operated by a woman in the lower floor of the Block House. She did not mention the woman's name, although she did mention her rent as being four dollars per month, not five dollars as Sibby Powers later claimed in 1894.[96] Lee's daughters also mentioned the woman with the candy store in their 1943 interviews, providing her name and the time in which she would have occupied the Block House. This woman's name was not Sibby Powers but rather "Mrs. Flaherty," and she lived in the Block House "before, during, and after the time" in which the Lee family would have occupied the upstairs room.[97]

If the seventy-year-old Lee sisters' memories served them correctly, then Sibby Powers had to be wrong in 1894 when she told the *Post* reporter that she had lived in the Block House for twenty-five years. In fact, nothing can be found in either city directories or census records to prove that an "S. Powers" or a "Sibby Powers" lived in the Point District proper for twenty-five years let alone in the Block House. There is a listing of a "Powers, S, Candy Store, Rental" in the 1878 *Confidential Business Report of Pittsburgh and Allegheny*, but it does not state where the store is located.[98] Assuming that this listing is, in fact, for Sibby Powers's store at the Block House, it still does not support her claim of having lived there for twenty-five years. It also does not support the Lee sisters' claim of Mrs. Flaherty operating the store.

The 1880 census stirs the pot even further. While it lists Hannah Lee and her daughters as living in Point Alley, it does not mention anyone by the name of Sibby Powers. The only Powers entry that comes close is that of Irishwoman Sarah Powers, living in 5 Fort Street with her husband, Peter, and their three children. The only thing in common between Sibby Powers and Sarah Powers is that both of their names begin with the letter S. Sarah

Powers is listed as being forty-four years old, which would place her at the age of fifty-eight by 1894. Sibby Powers said in her interview that she was over sixty years old. Sarah's husband is alive in 1880, whereas Sibby claimed that her husband passed away as early as 1859—and she did not mention any children. Finally, although 5 Fort Street would have been very close to the Block House, it is not necessarily the actual Block House, especially since Hannah Lee is listed as Point Alley, not Fort Street. Fort Street (originally named Point Street and later First Street) ran parallel to Point Alley, and the two streets were on either side of the Block House.[99]

And what about "Mrs. Flaherty"? Whereas Powers women are few and far between in both city directories and census records, many Flaherty women can be found beginning as early as 1861 and lasting into 1894. There were a number of different Flaherty families living at the Point during the nineteenth century, and many of them were related. The earliest female Flaherty listed in a city directory is Sabina P. Flaherty, seamstress, living in the rear of 23 Point Street in 1861. Sabina Flaherty is listed again in 1863 as the widow of Michael, living in the rear of 22 Duquesne Street (two blocks down from the Block House property). Interestingly, there is another Irish widow listed as living in the rear of 22 Duquesne Street in 1863—her name is Bridget Powers. The next mention of a Flaherty widow is in 1872, although this time it is Marie Flaherty, widow of Mike, living in "Old Fort Duquesne." Was Marie Flaherty also Sabina Flaherty? It would seem unlikely. The larger question here is the Old Fort Duquesne mention. It was common during the nineteenth century to refer to the Block House as "Old Fort Duquesne" or the remains of Fort Duquesne (an obvious mistake). Was Marie Flaherty living in the Block House in 1872?

Marie Flaherty aside, the connections between Sabina Flaherty and Sibby Powers are interesting. Sabina Flaherty comes up again and again in city directories during the nineteenth century. In 1878, she is living at 27 First Street (formerly Point Street). Four years later, she is still living in the same street—now renamed Fort Street—but she is listed as house no. 30 instead of 27. Sabina is still living in 30 Fort Street by 1889, only now she is specifically listed as living in the rear of the property. The 1892 directory is when it starts to get really interesting—and complicated. There are two people listed as living in the rear of 30 Fort Street. The first is Sabina Flaherty, widow of Michael, and the second person is Sarah Costello, widow of John. This is interesting because it is known for certain that Sarah Costello was the last person to live in the upstairs of the Block House. Sarah Costello is listed as living in the rear of 30 Fort Street from 1892 until 1894, the year in

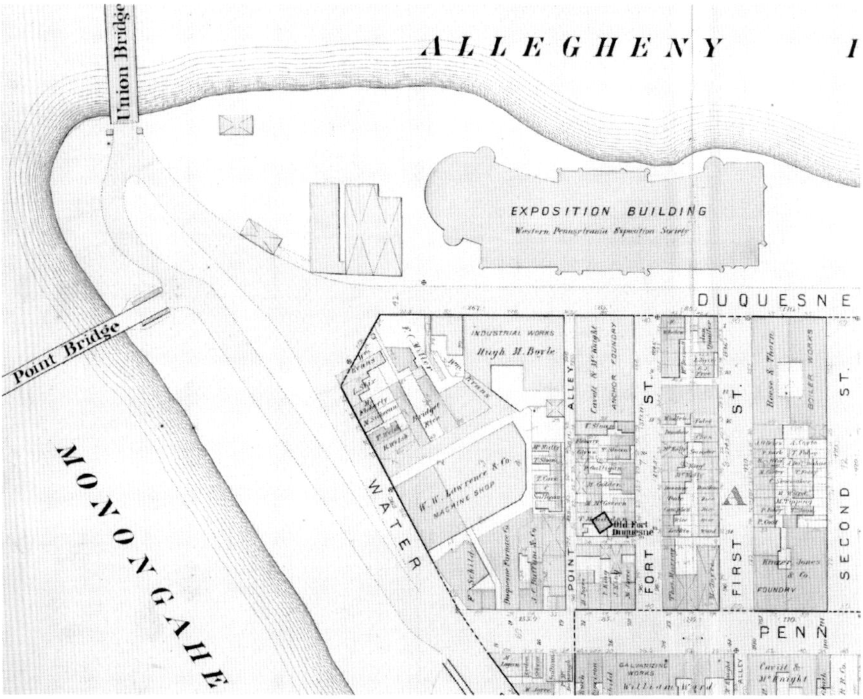

By 1889, the Point had grown with even more housing and industry. The Block House is shown but mistakenly listed as "Old Fort Duquesne." *Courtesy of G.M. Hopkins Maps Collections, Archive Service Center, University of Pittsburgh.*

which the Block House was turned over to the Daughters of the American Revolution. This could mean that the address for the Block House—or at least the upstairs room—was "the rear of #30 Fort Street." The only other person listed as living in the rear of 30 Fort Street from 1892 to 1894 is none other than Sabina Flaherty. In fact, the 1893 directory lists her as operating a candy store!

Were Sabina Flaherty and Sibby Powers the same person? The evidence is there: Irish women, widows since the early 1860s, possibly living in the Block House since the 1870s, operating candy stores, sharing similar first names (Sibby could easily have been a nickname for Sabina). There is the testimony of the Lee sisters, claiming that a Mrs. Flaherty operated a candy store below them in the 1880s. The only obstacle to the theory that Sabina Flaherty and Sibby Powers were one in the same is the difference in their surnames. Why would Sabina be listed as a Flaherty only to call herself Powers in later interviews? Was "Powers" her maiden name? Sabina is listed as "widow of Michael" as early as 1863. The 1857 and 1858 directories list Michael Flaherty as a laborer living in a house located at 23 Point Street—the same address used by Sabina P. Flaherty, seamstress, in the 1861 directory. Could Sabina have been a widow as early as 1861? If so that would provide even further evidence that she could, in fact, be Sibby Powers since Sibby claimed in 1894 that her husband died around 1859.[100]

In a 1933 article featured in the *Pittsburgh Press*, Sarah Costello's daughter, Delia Costello Smith, remembered Aunt Sibby Powers living below her and her mother in the Block House. Smith described her as "an old Irish lady."[101] Lois Wirth, a young woman writing an essay for the *Pittsburgh Post-Gazette* in 1935, remembered the stories her grandmother told her about growing up in the Point. Her grandmother specifically recalled how the Block House was "turned into a little candy-store owned by an aged lady named Mrs. Sibby. The children loved old Mrs. Sibby as well as her candy."[102] David L. Lawrence, former Pittsburgh mayor and governor of Pennsylvania, was born and raised in the Point District in the late nineteenth century. Interviewed in 1963 when he was in his seventies, Lawrence still had childhood memories of the Block House and Sibby Powers, stating that "we kids used to play in [the Block House] and around there. I remember one time an old lady named Powers moved in there & squatted, opened up a candy store and lived there."[103] The truth may never be known about Sibby Powers, but she has become a legend in Block House and Point District history. A replica of her window candy store is on display inside the Block House today as a testimony not only to her but also to the many other families who lived there as well.

CHANGES AND ADDITIONS

When the Block House officially became used as a residence, changes were made to its physical appearance. Some of these changes may have occurred as early as the 1770s, when it was in use as a trading post. There are no known images of the Block House from the time of the Craig family's inhabitance, but there is an image from 1832 that has helped considerably in understanding how the Block House was physically changed into a residential structure. This painting, made by Russell Smith, is the oldest known original image of the Block House.

The artwork shows the brick addition built by Turnbull, Marmie & Company in 1785. The large house with its gabled roof rises up behind the

This oil painting is an exact copy of an 1832 watercolor sketch by Russell Smith. The watercolor is the earliest known original image of the Block House. Painted in 1832, it depicts the Block House in use as a residence, with the Isaac Craig House standing directly behind the Block House. Smith created the oil painting years later in 1884. *Courtesy of the Catherine R. Miller Collection of Chatham University.*

Block House. The Block House is depicted with a chimney coming out of the point of the building (facing toward the three rivers at the Point). The chimney connected to a fireplace on the first floor of the Block House. Brick remains of the fireplace were unearthed during an archaeological dig in 2003, revealing their age to be anywhere from the mid- to late eighteenth century.[104] This could mean that the fireplace was there before people began to live in the Block House; however, considering that the Block House was originally a defensive military structure, it is highly unlikely that the fireplace was there prior to 1772 (when the building was converted into a trading post).

The drawing also shows a simple wooden lean-to shed attached to the western wall of the Block House. Its eastern back wall has two windows cut into the bricks in the center of the wall. One window is for the first floor, and it sits directly on top of one of the gun loop timbers. This window is approximately where the modern entrance door to the Block House is located. The other window is on the second floor. Unlike the lower window, this opening actually eliminates one of the gun loop timbers.

The southern sidewall features some notable changes as well. In 1832, the original door is still in place underneath the lower gun loops, but two windows have been added. One window is on the first floor, eliminating one of the wooden gun loop timbers. The other window is located on the second floor directly above the first window—gun loops have also been removed to make way for this opening. Both windows appear to be double-paned. Perhaps one of the most interesting features is located at the top center of this southern wall. It is a small, rectangular stone tablet reading, "A.D. 1764 ~ Coll. Bouquet." The date obviously represents the year in which the Block House was constructed, while "Coll. Bouquet" refers to Colonel Henry Bouquet, the officer in charge of Fort Pitt at the time of the building's construction. This is the same stone tablet viewed by Watson in 1804 and Lyford in 1836; it is also in the same location in which they would have seen the tablet.[105]

The interior of the Block House also changed, although there are no existing paintings, drawings or photographs of the interior of the building from the eighteenth and nineteenth centuries. On the first floor, there was the fireplace in the "point" of the building, as evidenced by the exterior chimney in the Smith painting and by the brick remains from the 2003 dig. Near the interior southern sidewall, there was an opening in the second floor for a ladder to gain access to the upper room. This ladder was used by the soldiers as well as by families later in the nineteenth century. A small wooden beam was placed between two of the upper floor joists at the opening for the ladder. This beam was beveled so that the soldiers could clear the opening with their muskets on their backs while using the ladder. The beveled beam can still be seen today inside the Block House.

As mentioned earlier in the chapter, the Block House experienced even more change in the 1840s when it was converted into a multi-family dwelling. These changes are most notable in an original drawing by Sherman Day in his *Historical Collections of the State of Pennsylvania* from 1843. The brick house addition can still be seen in the background, and the Block House chimney remains in the same location as in 1832. The two windows on the southern sidewall are also still present, including the stone tablet; however, the original door entrance is gone. A small staircase is placed directly in front of where the door used to be, with a gun loop timber serving as the top step to the staircase. The stairs lead to a new doorway cut into the brick wall of the second floor of the Block House. This door is where the second-floor family would have entered the building. The western wall still has a lean-to, but instead of being a simple shed, it is an actual addition, with a doorway, a

Redoubt at Pittsburg.

This sketch from 1843 depicts the Block House after it became a multi-family tenement. Note the upper door opening for the second-floor family's access. *From Sherman Day's* Historical Collections of the State of Pennsylvania *(1843).*

window and a chimney. The lean-to addition served as the entrance to the lower floor of the Block House. A notable feature of Day's drawing is his depiction of the eastern back wall of the building. It clearly shows a door cut into the same area in which a window was located in the 1832 Smith drawing. The door also looks similar to the building's modern door entrance. Despite this similarity, it is believed that the door in the Day drawing was made through artistic license.

Now that the Block House was an apartment with two separate families, the downstairs family could no longer access the upstairs room—at least not from inside. This meant that the indoor ladder leading up to the second floor had to be removed. If the first-floor inhabitants wished to visit the second-floor inhabitants, they had to walk outside to the exterior staircase on the southern sidewall and enter through the door at the top of the stairs. Upon opening the door they would have faced a landing with a smaller set of steps leading into the upper level of the Block House. According to the Lee sisters' interview with Bliss:

> *The upper floor was divided into two rooms by a partition. Steps led up to a doorway cut through the brick wall of the redoubt, the sill of the door resting directly on the timbers through which the port holes had been cut. Just inside this door was a small vestibule with three steps leading up to the second floor.*[106]

The partitioning of the second floor did not necessarily mean an actual wall partition; it could have been something as simple as a curtain. The sisters do not mention how they heated the upper room or how they cooked their food (since the fireplace was located downstairs).

The only walls that are not visible in any images from the nineteenth century are the northern sidewall and the northwestern wall. This is somewhat frustrating because these are the walls that directly faced the brick house addition built long ago by Turnbull & Company. It is unknown whether the brick house was ever physically attached to the Block House. During the time of Isaac Craig, the brick house and the Block House were part of one housing unit; in other words, the family who lived in the brick addition also utilized the Block House structure. This would imply that the two buildings were connected in some way, but there is nothing to confirm this idea. The Block House eventually became its own separate living space apart from the brick addition by the 1830s (if not earlier). Years later, when the Block House was undergoing restoration, a significant amount of renovation had to be completed on these two walls in comparison to the rest of the building. In fact, the entire corner where the two walls connect have restored gun loop timbers, a majority of restored bricks and restored roofing elements at the top of the structure. It almost seems as though an opening of some kind did exist in this area—why else would there be so much restoration?

Once again, the Lee sisters shed some light on the mystery by mentioning that the upstairs room of the Block House had three windows. The first window was located directly above the modern door entrance (already known), and the second window was located on the southern wall facing Penn Avenue (also already known). The third window was "in the back of the redoubt on the right hand side of the wall facing the building to the rear. This building (the original Isaac Craig residence), at the rear, was only about four feet from the redoubt, steps led up to the second floor of this building between it and the redoubt."[107]

The Lee sisters provide a lot of information here, and yet so much is left for discussion. The existence of the third window confirms that the northern sidewall and northwestern wall had to be restored to a certain extent. The

The Block House as it appeared in about 1854. This drawing was published in *Harper's Weekly* in 1854 as a reproduction of an original sketch by the artist John M. Falconer. Different versions of Falconer's sketch were produced by other artists throughout the nineteeth century. *From* Harper's Weekly *(1854).*

proximity of the Isaac Craig building and the Block House also leads to the speculation that maybe they were, in fact, attached at some point in time. When the Block House was restored in 1894, the third window was mentioned in the meeting minutes of the Daughters of the American Revolution; one of the members suggested that the window was original to the structure. Given what we now know about the building, this is obviously not true, although it is interesting to note that out of all of the windows in the Block House at that time, this particular window seemed "original."[108]

In January 1854, the artist John M. Falconer visited the Point in search of remains from Fort Pitt and Fort Duquesne. He made a watercolor and graphite image of the Block House depicting a woman entering the upper floor of the building from an exterior staircase. This image was reproduced as an engraving for an article in *Harper's Weekly* magazine in December 1858, and it was copied by Jacob Beeson in an engraving for the *Pittsburgh Leader Almanac* of 1872.[109] Both the original Falconer depiction and its subsequent copies show a Block House heading toward deterioration. It appears to be poorly maintained and surrounded by dilapidated structures. Assuming that Day's image was fairly accurate (aside from the extra door), it could be said that the Block House's condition worsened considerably in a little over ten years. Would the Fort Pitt Block House survive another century?

Chapter 3

Schenley, the DAR and the Block House

They planned for vandalism—we for patriotism. Patriotism wins.

As the nineteenth century came to a close, it seemed that the Block House was not likely to survive much longer due to its deteriorated condition. Many different persons and groups approached the owner of the Block House, Mary Elizabeth Croghan Schenley, in efforts to save the structure and open it as a historic site. For various reasons, these requests were consistently denied until 1892, when she suddenly gave the building to the newly formed Pittsburgh Chapter of the Daughters of the American Revolution (DAR). The DAR's plans included restoring the Block House to its original 1764 appearance and opening it to the public free of charge. No sooner did it fulfill such plans than it was faced with a new threat: the transformation of the Point District into an industrialized rail yard. Fighting city officials, powerful businessmen and huge corporations, the DAR was ultimately successful in saving the building it treasured so much—the Fort Pitt Block House.

The Deterioration of the Block House

Many journalists and historians visited the Fort Pitt Block House throughout the nineteenth century to see the last remaining structure of Fort Pitt. The days of British and French soldiers and Indian warfare began to be romanticized in true Victorian fashion, with the Block House becoming more and more symbolic of the region's early history. By the late nineteenth century, however, the Block House had also begun to show its age. People who sublet the building, such as Sibby Powers and Hannah Lee, obviously could not afford to keep the structure in good condition, and the property's lease owners did nothing to improve the site.

There were also no attempts by the Block House's actual owner, Mary Elizabeth Croghan Schenley, to restore and preserve the historic structure—at least not until much later in her life. Schenley was none other than the same Mary Elizabeth Croghan mentioned earlier, the granddaughter of James O'Hara who inherited the Point District following the death of her mother in 1827. As she grew older, she became one of the most eligible heiresses in Pittsburgh. Her father, William Croghan, did his best to raise his daughter on his own, but when she turned fifteen, he decided to send her to a prestigious boarding school in New York City. At this school, she met and fell in love with the English captain Edward W. Schenley, nearly twenty years her senior. The couple eloped to Britain, where they were soon married. Choked with anger, embarrassment and grief, Mary's father tried in vain to stop the elopement and its exposure, but it was no use—the couple was now living in London, and the scandal spread through Pittsburgh society like wildfire.

Mary Schenley eventually reconciled with her father and returned to Pittsburgh with her new family to live at the Croghan mansion. The Schenley family did not stay long, however, as Captain Schenley did not like Pittsburgh or its "backwoods" society. Soon after they returned to England, Mary's father died—supposedly of a broken heart. In his will, he mandated that the Croghan mansion be kept in exact order in case Mary or her children ever decided to return. Mary did come back to the house occasionally, with her last visit to her childhood home taking place in 1863. She would never return again. Spending the remainder of her life in Britain and France, Schenley most likely never visited the Point District, let alone the Block House.[110]

The condition of the Point and its historic structure became noticeable to visitors of the city, as well as its inhabitants. Passing through on his way home from California in 1889, English traveler Samuel Storey visited Pittsburgh with special intentions of viewing the remains of Fort Pitt. Encountering the Block House as so many others had before him, Storey made the following comment:

> *Not to the public buildings or great industrial works of the city, but to the remains of this fort, was my first visit made. Fort in the real sense there*

> *is none, but amongst the narrow and tortuous streets of what is now the poorest part of Pittsburgh an old ramshackle red-brick house stands as its only surviving relic. The stone which used to adorn the wall, and records name and date, has been removed to the City Hall. It was curious to stand in the midst of great industrious communities and think that little more than a century ago here, amidst boundless forests and howling Indians, the French, in their struggle for colonial empire, boldly planted themselves—the French first and then the British.*[111]

Unfortunately, Storey was not embellishing his surroundings or the condition of the Block House. Although many recognized the historical importance of the Block House, the structure remained just another run-down tenement in the middle of the Point. Journalists' depictions of the Point and the Block House grew increasingly critical of the deplorable living conditions in the district and the deterioration of the last remnant of Fort Pitt. Storey mentioned in his brief description that the famous stone tablet located in the Block House's southern sidewall had been removed to city hall. This was done in 1872 when the tablet was placed inside Pittsburgh's new city hall building on Smithfield Street.[112] According to a commemorative publication on the city hall, the tablet was placed in the building's stairwell underneath a window depicting the Block House and the city's seal. The stone was "taken out of the walls of the old redoubt, and built into the wall here [city hall] for preservation, to show that Pittsburgh has a history."[113]

There were some efforts to save the building from deterioration, most notably by Pittsburgh resident Frederick T. Gretton. Gretton was born and raised in England, immigrating to the United States in the early 1880s. He was eventually hired as the chief chemist for Jones & Laughlin Steel Corporation in Pittsburgh. Making his home in the "Steel City," Gretton fell in love with its arts and history. He had an especial affection for the Block House, and beginning in 1888, he tried for years to save it from destruction. Working with the British American Association, he lobbied the Schenley estate for preservation of the Block House. The response was disappointing; the estate would not consider giving up the building or preserving it due to leases on the structure by the families living in it. These leases would not expire until 1891, thereby blocking Gretton's attempts to restore the historic building.[114] The Fort Pitt Block House remained in a state of decline.

A NEW CHAPTER FORMS

A new chapter in Block House history began with the formation of another "chapter"—the Pittsburgh Chapter of the Daughters of the American Revolution. The chapter was founded in June 1891 by a group of wealthy Pittsburgh women who could trace their ancestry to veterans and participants from the American Revolution. The National Society of the Daughters of the American Revolution had been organized less than a year earlier in October 1890. The Daughters of the American Revolution (DAR) was formed as a result of another organization, the Sons of the American Revolution, denying women the right to join its membership. The DAR allowed membership for any woman who could directly trace her ancestry to someone who contributed to or fought for the Patriot side in the American Revolution. Various chapters throughout the United States quickly formed during the late nineteenth and early twentieth centuries.

The era in which groups like the DAR were formed was an interesting time in the nation's history, as well as in Pittsburgh's history. Large waves of immigrants from Europe, Asia and beyond were flooding into the United States, bringing new languages, ideas and cultures. An unfounded fear of losing American ideals and culture spread throughout the nation. Suddenly it became necessary to instill a sense of patriotism to the United States and its history, and this was mainly done through education, historic preservation and commemoration activities. According to the proceedings from the DAR's inaugural meeting in October 1890, the overall purpose of the DAR was "to teach patriotism by erecting monuments and protecting historical spots, by observing historical anniversaries, by promoting the cause of education, especially the study of history, the enlightenment of the foreign population, and all that makes for good citizenship."[115]

It can be stated fairly, then, that the purpose behind the formation of the Pittsburgh Chapter DAR was to protect and promote the history of Pittsburgh, especially during a time when that history seemed lost to the public mind. The chapter fulfilled its purpose by installing historical plaques and markers throughout the city, celebrating national holidays such as Flag Day, and most importantly, saving Pittsburgh's oldest and most treasured structure, the Fort Pitt Block House.

THE FORT PITT SOCIETY

The first meeting of the chapter took place on June 10, 1891, with the chapter's charter being officially accepted into the NSDAR by November of that same year. It is not clear from the chapter's meeting minutes and other records whether the Block House was the actual reason for starting the organization, but it was certainly on the top of its list from the very beginning, for the chapter began sending requests for the Block House property to Mary Schenley as early as spring 1892.[116] One of the chapter's founding members, Amelia Neville Shields Oliver, was chosen to send the official request to Schenley. Oliver had strong ties to the Block House's history, being a great-granddaughter of Isaac Craig as well as a great-great-granddaughter of John Neville. Her letter to Schenley noted the following:

> *I have been appointed by* [the Pittsburgh Chapter] *to write you in regard to the restoration and improvement of the old Block House, or redoubt, built by Colonel Boquet* [sic] *in 1764...One of the objects of our Society is the acquisition and preservation of historical places and buildings, of which we have so few in America...*[The Block House] *is a place of great interest to all Pittsburghers, but particularly to our Society, many of whose ancestors were stationed at this Fort during the wars with the Indians and French, and during the Revolutionary War.*[117]

The request clearly defines what the DAR's intentions were with the Block House and why the organization felt it important to save it from destruction. Many of the women who made up the Pittsburgh Chapter were similar to Amelia Oliver in that they were direct descendants of early Pittsburgh residents like Isaac Craig and James O'Hara. As Oliver alluded in her letter, the Block House was a symbol of early Pittsburgh history, as well as a symbol of personal histories for chapter members.

The correspondence also revealed that Schenley had previously attempted to "save" the Block House by offering it to the City of Pittsburgh; however, the city wanted additional property surrounding the building. Schenley, acting on the advice of her estate agent, refused to give the property, allowing for the deal with the city to fall through. The Pittsburgh Chapter, via Oliver's request, also asked for a small amount of property surrounding the Block House so that the entire site could be made into a park. Oliver stated that the director of public works for the City of Pittsburgh, Edward Bigelow, assured

Mary Elizabeth Croghan Schenley in her later years. This portrait was given to the Fort Pitt Society of the Daughters of the American Revolution by Schenley's estate agent, John W. Herron. *Courtesy of the Fort Pitt Society Collections.*

the chapter that Point Alley or Fort Street would be widened (allowing for better access to the Block House site) if the DAR should get the property. The chapter itself wanted the proposed park to stretch from Penn Avenue to Duquesne Way. Finally, Oliver offered Schenley an honorary lifetime membership in the Pittsburgh Chapter and requested a portrait of Schenley to hang inside the Block House once it became open to the public.[118]

The ladies received a response from Schenley in a letter dated May 23, 1892, through which she gave her consent to bestow the Block House to the Pittsburgh Chapter NSDAR. She also agreed to give them a small amount of ground surrounding the building; however, she could not provide them with the exact amount until she conferred with her estate agent, Colonel William A. Herron of W.A. Herron & Sons of Pittsburgh. Schenley willingly accepted the offer of DAR membership and promised to send the chapter her portrait so that it could be displayed inside the Block House. It was at the chapter's one-year anniversary meeting on June 10, 1892, that Amelia Neville Shields Oliver formally announced the gifting of the Block House to the chapter from Mary Schenley.[119]

The next letter from Schenley came in August 1892, and it provided more exact terms for the Block House and surrounding property, stating, "I have now written to Mr. Herron requesting him to prepare the deed giving to the association the old Fort with 80 feet on the new street, running back 80 or 90 feet—I hope this will be satisfactory." The new street mentioned in the letter was O'Hara Avenue, a street proposed by Edward Bigelow. Bigelow had persuaded Schenley to allow for the new street to run through her property at the Point. The avenue would be placed between Duquesne Way and Penn Avenue, running parallel to the two streets. The already existing Fort Street would be widened, and Point Alley would eventually be closed completely. The street closures and additions worked well with the Pittsburgh Chapter's plans since access points to the Block House could be placed on Fort Street and the new O'Hara Avenue, thus making it easier to visit the site.[120]

Although the Block House was now promised to the Pittsburgh Chapter, the organization could not legally own the property unless it became incorporated under state law. A meeting was held on September 23, 1892, to take action on securing a charter of incorporation for the Pittsburgh Chapter NSDAR. It was decided that the incorporated name would be the Daughters of the American Revolution of Allegheny County, Pennsylvania. Any member of the Pittsburgh Chapter NSDAR was automatically a member of the DAR of Allegheny County, and a board of directors was selected from the chapter to oversee all activities and projects relating to the Block House. Directors were elected by the chapter every so many years; officers for the board of directors were elected by the board members themselves. The first directors for the board of the Daughters of the American Revolution of Allegheny County were Julia K. Hogg, Anne McDowell Price Childs, Matilda Wilkins Denny, Henrietta Logan Scott, Emily Black Moorhead, Margaret Irwin Hays, Amelia Neville Shields Oliver, Mary Lothrop Painter and Carrie Morehead Holland.[121]

The official incorporation of the Daughters of the American Revolution of Allegheny County, Pennsylvania, was recorded on November 12, 1892, with the purpose of "maintaining private parks in which to preserve the Block House." This name remained in use until June 1917, when it was legally changed to the Fort Pitt Society of the Daughters of the American Revolution of Allegheny County, Pennsylvania—the name still used by the organization today. For sake of clarity, the name "Fort Pitt Society" will be used throughout the rest of this book when referring to those women who worked to save and protect the Fort Pitt Block House.[122]

GETTING THE BLOCK HOUSE

It seemed as if everything was in place to formally receive the Block House—Schenley had given consent, and the Pittsburgh Chapter had successfully become incorporated to own the property—and yet the Fort Pitt Society did not receive the deed until April 1894. It is clearly stated in meeting minutes from September 1892 that the deed was to be sent by April 1894; however, separate minutes from a meeting held on October 11, 1893, show that the ladies were expecting the deed to arrive any day. They even seemed irritated that the deed had not yet arrived. By November, inquiries were made to Thomas D. Carnahan, Schenley's personal attorney and the assistant attorney for the City of Pittsburgh, as to when the deed would be delivered to the Fort Pitt Society. Carnahan replied that he did not have the deed nor did he know when it would be finalized; he believed that the deed was actually in the hands of Herron & Sons. When contacted by the ladies, Herron & Sons claimed that Carnahan had the deed. This runaround between lawyers and estate agents was extremely frustrating to the society, so much so that by early December 1893, members had hired their own lawyer, J. Harvey White, to push the matter forward.[123]

At the same time that they hired White, the ladies received a letter from Herron & Sons. The estate agents had caught wind that the ladies were upset and wanted to resolve any issues between them. Addressed to the society's president, Matilda Denny, the letter provided an explanation for the delay and the confusion. First, the senior partner of the firm and the one in charge of the Schenley estate, W.A. Herron, had been ill for an extended period of time and therefore unable to attend to business. Secondly, the firm was not aware that the DAR had actually secured a charter of incorporation for owning the Block House property. Finally, the agents were still waiting for the official location of O'Hara Avenue by the City of Pittsburgh. When the Fort Pitt Society asked Schenley for the Block House property in 1892, Edward Bigelow had already presented a plan to Herron & Sons for the opening of O'Hara Avenue with the eventual vacation of all streets in the Point District. Only Penn Avenue, Duquesne Way and the proposed O'Hara Avenue would remain. Shortly after this, Herron & Sons received notification from Schenley regarding the allotment of the Block House and some surrounding property to the DAR. In this same correspondence, Schenley also informed her estate agents that Bigelow had visited her in London, showing her the same plan that he presented to Herron & Sons weeks before.

When Bigelow met again with Herron & Sons, he suggested that the property given to the DAR should front on the proposed O'Hara Avenue,

This is one of the earliest known photographic images of the Block House, taken by Theodore F. Brown in about 1890. The identities of the woman and children in the image are unknown; the woman may be Sarah Costello, who lived in the upstairs room of the Block House in the 1890s. Note the condition of the Block House and its surroundings. *Courtesy of the Pennsylvania Department of the Carnegie Library of Pittsburgh.*

with a piece of property extending back to take in the actual Block House structure. Bigelow assured Herron & Sons that he would have an ordinance for locating O'Hara Avenue prepared and handed to city councils as soon as possible. In its letter to the Fort Pitt Society, Herron & Sons explained that the ordinance was not presented to the council until September 1893; it also admitted that it was not sure if the ordinance had even been passed by council. Because the ordinance had not been passed, Herron & Sons decided to wait until O'Hara Avenue was formally located by the City of Pittsburgh before allotting the Block House property.[124]

Based on meeting minutes and correspondence mentioned previously, it is clear that the ladies not only knew of Bigelow's and Schenley's plans for the Point but approved of them, too. As long as O'Hara Avenue was opened, it did not matter if Fort Street was eventually closed. In the eyes of the Fort Pitt Society, the closing and vacating of streets at the Point would only serve to help preserve the Block House—perhaps a larger park could eventually be constructed in the Point to commemorate early Pittsburgh history! In any case, Herron's letter must have served its purpose in satisfying the DAR's questions, for no more mention was made in meeting minutes or correspondence of the deed fiasco.

The ordinance allowing for the location of O'Hara Avenue was eventually passed by city councils. This ordinance only provided a physical location for the street, not for its actual opening. Now that the street was located, the property for the Block House could be officially drawn up in a deed. It was finally signed by Mary Schenley at her villa in Cannes, France, on March 15, 1894. Arriving to the United States in April, the deed was formally recorded in the Allegheny County Courthouse on April 28, 1894. The Fort Pitt Society of the Daughters of the American Revolution was now the owner of the Block House.[125]

According to the deed's language, the Fort Pitt Society had to pay one dollar to Mary Schenley in order to own the Block House. The deed provided the society with the building itself and ninety feet by one hundred feet of property surrounding it, as well as a strip of property that extended from the Block House to Penn Avenue. This strip was twenty feet by ninety feet in size. Part of the ninety- by one-hundred-foot section of property encompassed parts of Point Alley and Fort Street. The back section of property faced O'Hara Avenue (which only existed on paper). The strip reaching out to Penn Avenue would allow for an entrance to the Block House site once Fort Street and Point Alley were closed.[126]

The next part of the deed was perhaps the most crucial in terms of the Fort Pitt Society's property rights. It stated that the deed was subject to

> [the] *right of the party of the first part* [Schenley] *to represent said above described real estate in all proceedings looking to the opening of O'Hara Avenue and the vacation of Fort Street and Point Alley, the purpose of the party of the first part being to retain, reserve and not part with the right to petition the City of Pittsburgh, in behalf of said real estate, to open said O'Hara Avenue and to vacate said Fort Street and Point Alley; and she hereby reserves said right to herself, her heirs, executors and administrators, without liability however, for any assessment of benefits on said real estate by reason of said opening or vacations.*[127]

This clause should have raised some concerns among the ladies since it essentially took away their property rights; however, the section of the deed that concerned them the most had to do with their ability to take care of the

Original watercolor of the Block House made in 1894, prior to its restoration by the Fort Pitt Society of the Daughters of the American Revolution. *Courtesy of the Fort Pitt Society Collections.*

historic structure. The society's mission with the Block House, as defined in the deed, was in "maintaining, preserving and keeping in good condition said 'Block House,' perpetuating the historical associations surrounding the same, improving and suitably maintaining the above described ground enclosing and about said 'Block House,' preserving archaeological remains[,] and promoting historical research."[128] The reversion clause of the deed declared that if at any point the Fort Pitt Society and its successors should prove unable to fulfill its mission of preserving and maintaining the Block House and its grounds for historical purposes, the Block House and property would immediately revert back to Mary Schenley and her heirs. Although the ladies feared such a reversion, they went forward with signing the deed, determined to make Mary Schenley and the citizens of Pittsburgh proud of their preservation efforts.

TENANTS TAKE THEIR LEAVE

The deed was signed, and the Fort Pitt Society was now the owner of the oldest building in Pittsburgh and the only original structure left of Fort Pitt. In accordance to their mission, the women set about planning for the building's restoration and opening to the public as a historical site and "museum of the colonial era." Before they could proceed with the restoration, however, they had to attend to another important matter: the tenants. Not only did the society have to evict and compensate the tenants of the Block House, but it also had to evict the other tenants living on the property. This included families living in the former Isaac Craig House.

In a letter written to the Fort Pitt Society's agent, Captain William F. Aull, William Herron provided the names of every single tenant on the property, as well as their monthly rents. A person named "T. Maddon," listed as living in McKees Rocks, was the lessee of the actual Block House building, as well as an adjoining shed and stable and nearby brick tenements. The subtenants of the Block House were, of course, Sibby Powers and Sarah Costello, listed as paying four dollars per month and five dollars per month, respectively. The Isaac Craig House was leased by "the Estate of B. Lamb"; it was subleased by "B. Dougherty" at four dollars per month, with the other apartments inside the house standing vacant.[129]

The DAR acquisition affected at least eighteen different lease owners and subtenants. Only two of the lease owners actually lived in their rentals; all other structures were occupied by subtenants. In the letter to Captain Aull, Herron made it clear that none of the lease owners were paid up in rent, with many still owing a considerable amount of money in rent and taxes. Because they were delinquent in their rent payments, Herron maintained that the lease owners did not have any rights to their properties. If any lease owner or tenant should argue otherwise and a settlement was reached by the society, that money should go directly to Mary Schenley until the rent and taxes owed to her estate were paid in full. Finally, all of the leases within the DAR's property expired on April 1, 1894, with full notice of eviction given in advance by Herron & Sons.

In a postscript, William Herron mentioned a house located within the twenty- by ninety-foot strip of property reaching to Penn Avenue. The house was leased by Peter King, who subleased it to a man named William Shriber. Herron stated that "Mr. King has one House…on the 20 ft on Penn Ave which I suppose can stand for the present as we want to get all that is due Mrs. Schenley after giving the Daughters of the American Revolution such a Handsome Gift." Aside from suggesting that the ladies give "all that is due" to Schenley, this letter also alludes to the purpose of having the strip of land in the first place: as an entrance to Penn Avenue once Fort Street and Point Alley were closed and O'Hara Avenue opened.[130]

Herron's letter prepared the ladies for the daunting task that they now faced: eviction. Evicting the tenants was not easy. Many families were upset—and reasonably so—at being forced to leave their homes, homes that they had lived in for years. They were faced with the expenses of moving as well as with the stress of finding new dwellings. There was also confusion among the tenants as to who exactly owned their houses and what they owed in rent. At the celebration held by the DAR in honor of receiving the deed to the Block

House, Fort Pitt Society president Matilda Denny stated, "We will have trouble getting these tenants out…They now refuse to leave until they can find a place elsewhere, and one woman absolutely claims she owns the blockhouse. We must not offend them or they might set fire to the old relic."[131] The woman Denny was referring to was none other than Sibby Powers.

As mentioned in the previous chapter, Powers was interviewed by Pittsburgh newspapers at this time since she was one of the last occupants of the Block House. Two articles were published in which she willingly voiced her opinions on being evicted. Days before she was scheduled to move out of the Block House, agents (either from Herron or Aull) stopped by to collect a final rent. Sibby exclaimed to the newspaper reporter, "And to think he wanted the rent…not a cent of rent he'll ever get now. Shure it's bad enough to pay when you're living right along in one place, but what do they expect when you've got to move out every stick of goods?"[132] Returning to a more somber demeanor, the old Irish widow made this remark:

> *I would be willing to keep on paying $5 a month for* [the apartment] *if they would only let me stay. I would die if I had to go anywhere else. There is no place for me and I have neither kith nor kin. The fine ladies will need someone to look after the place and they might keep me…I could get a room down around the corner, but the man wants $9 a month for and I could never pay the rent.*[133]

It was discovered later that Powers did, in fact, move to another tenement not far from the Block House. While never mentioning her new rent fee, she did comment on how the windows in her new home were not big enough to house her candy store as she did in the Block House.[134] It is presumed that Sibby Powers lived out the rest of her days in the Point District, selling candy to neighborhood children as a way to pay her rent.

The ladies did not allow Sibby Powers to stay, but they did allow another tenant to remain in exchange for taking care of the Block House. This tenant was Matthew Golden. Golden was technically a lease owner—one of the lease owners who actually occupied his property instead of subleasing it to others. The property was larger than most, and at least half of it rested on the Fort Pitt Society's property. This presented a problem since the ladies were intent on tearing down any structure (aside from the Block House) within their property lines, especially those closest to the Block House. Golden's home was farther down on Fort Street, above the Isaac Craig House. It was reported that he first began to lease his property in about 1878, paying

Another image of the Block House immediately before its restoration. The Isaac Craig House and other nearby structures that once surrounded the Block House have been demolished. *From* Report of the Commission to Locate the Frontier Forts of Pennsylvania, *vol. 2 (1896).*

$350 for the lease hold. Although his lease was originally for eight years, supposedly the agents of the Schenley estate told him that he could have the property as long as he wanted it. With this promise in mind, Golden added on to his house over the years. By 1894, he felt that he had "paid off" his home and was now the official owner—a mistaken belief. Disabled with rheumatism and having three children still living at home, Golden was shocked when he received an eviction notice in late March 1894.[135]

In the Fort Pitt Society's meeting minutes from May 14, 1894, the women discussed the issue of evicting the tenants. They mention one man in particular who refused to leave, claiming that he owned his house outright. Although his name is never mentioned, it is very likely that this tenant was Golden. Whoever he was, the ladies ultimately decided to give him $200 in damages. This was a significant amount of money considering that the other tenants received the equivalent of one month's rent (typically $4 or $5). Even if Golden was not the tenant who received $200, an agreement was reached in which the DAR hired Golden to take care of the Block House, thereby enabling him to remain on his property.[136]

THE RESTORATION OF THE BLOCK HOUSE

The caretaker secured, the ladies moved on to the actual restoration of the Block House and its grounds. As stated previously, the Fort Pitt Society wanted all surrounding structures removed from the property so that the Block House could be in a more park-like setting. The ladies also wanted the building to look as original as possible. The dilapidated tenement houses next to it detracted from its history and appearance, and these structures would have to be removed. Despite this, much discussion was made as to whether or not the Isaac Craig House should be left standing. This home was important to the ladies in many ways. Built in 1785, it was one of the oldest buildings in Pittsburgh. It was also the ancestral home of many Pittsburgh Chapter DAR members, including Amelia Neville Shields Oliver, who especially lobbied for its restoration. The following account provides the exact reasoning as to why the house was ultimately removed:

> *Some discussion was had as to the preservation of the brick building adjoining the Block House, which is about twenty years more recent date than the Block House & was occupied by the family of Maj. Craig. Mrs. Oliver was in favor of restoring this old house, as it might prove useful to the Society for meetings & could be also made available as a place of residence for the person or persons who may, hereafter be placed in charge of the Block House. Mrs. B.H. Painter moved that we abide by our full decision to demolish all of the surrounding buildings, this being seconded was also carried. The expense of fixing up this house was our one objection to perpetuating it and it was thought too that its proximity to the Block House would detract from the appearance of the building & further more Miss Denny reported that the work of removal was already in progress.*[137]

The Fort Pitt Society removed more than ten buildings from the property, including the Isaac Craig House. The ladies set about hiring an architect and engineer to conduct the restoration on the Block House. It is not clear from meeting minutes or surviving documents how much it cost to restore the building. A news article published on June 12, 1894, claimed that the restoration cost $4,000, with $1,300 donated to the project.[138] This claim is most likely accurate, although it is known that the ladies eventually received numerous donations, including an anonymous gift of $2,000.[139] The restoration itself was not well documented, but recent condition reports on the structure provide clues on what was restored and how the process was carried out. Any windows or door openings were filled in with replacement bricks, stone and wood. All replacement bricks used in the restoration were taken from the Isaac Craig House, which was known to have been constructed with bricks from Fort Pitt. This meant that all bricks in the Block House following the restoration were made at the fort in the eighteenth century; however, they were not all original to the building. It is unknown just where the Fort Pitt Society obtained the replacement stone and wood.

The gun loops had to be replaced in areas where they were missing, as well as in areas where there was a significant amount of rotting. The ladies and their architect were very careful in mandating that each new gun loop be made to look exactly like the original. This effort was done fairly well, as even today visitors cannot initially determine the difference between the original and replacement gun loops. Although the restoration was successful in replicating the look of the original gun loops, the way in which the wood was replaced and repaired was not always done soundly. In one area, the original gun loop was cut in half by a door opening. When filling in the opening, the original half was conjoined with a replacement half. Over the years, these two halves have increasingly separated, causing potential issues in the brick walls sitting above them.[140]

The stone foundation exterior wall was entirely repointed with a Portland cement mix, leaving the exterior stonework in high relief. It is not exactly clear if this is how the building's exterior stone would have originally appeared. The interior stone wall was repointed in some areas, but so much repointing has occurred over the last hundred years that it is hard to determine how much of it was done in the 1894 restoration. Exterior corners of the stone wall were reinforced with bricks; it can be assumed that these were the same bricks taken from the Isaac Craig House. Brick-reinforced exterior corners most likely would not have been original features to the Block House. As mentioned earlier, all replacement bricks for the upper walls and elsewhere were taken from the Isaac Craig House. In most areas where mortar repair and/or replacement were needed on the brick walls, a type of mortar was used that was similar to the original used in 1764. Although the mortar used was appropriate for preservation efforts, the way in which the mortar was tooled in the joints was more standard for mortar work in the nineteenth century than the eighteenth century. That being said, it is hard for the untrained eye to distinguish between the original brick mortar and the restored mortar.[141]

Around the exterior of the Block House, there are six metal discs attached to the brick walls of the building. These discs are connected to six steel bolts

Postcard image of the Block House shortly after it was restored in 1894. One can see where sections of the brick walls had to be replaced with bricks from the Isaac Craig House; the metal discs installed to lend support to the building are also visible in this image. *Courtesy of the Fort Pitt Society Collections.*

that were placed into the brick walls of the Block House in an attempt to provide more stabilization. Two were installed on the building's north wall, two on the south wall and one bolt on each western wall. Inside the Block House, these bolts become metal bars attached to some of the wooden joists of the upper floor. Following a study on the building in 2011, it was found that these steel reinforcements do not provide as much stability to the Block House as previously thought; however, since it would do more harm than good to remove them, the steel bolts remain in place as a testimony to the early preservation efforts of the Fort Pitt Society.[142]

The final piece of the restoration came with the return of the stone tablet from the city hall building. The society petitioned the City of Pittsburgh for the replacement of the tablet to its rightful position within the walls of the Block House. The petition was approved in December 1894, along with approval for the Block House to be exempt from property taxes. The tablet was officially returned and reinstalled in the Block House in January 1895.[143] Although early images of the building clearly show the tablet at the top of the structure's south wall, the society placed it above the new door opening on the Block House's eastern wall. This opening would serve as the official entrance to the building. A new staircase leading to the upstairs room was placed inside the Block House within its westernmost corner. Although the staircase and door entrance were not original features or in original locations, the majority of the Block House now looked almost exactly as it did in 1764. It was ready to be opened to the public as an official historical site.

THE CALM BEFORE THE STORM

With the restoration completed, the Block House was opened to the public as a historical site and museum by July 1895. The first seven years of the Fort Pitt Society's ownership were relatively peaceful. A small collection of artifacts given to the society over the years was put on display inside the Block House, and Golden and his family were on duty to provide tours and information to visitors. One of the most interesting artifacts on display was an old stone sundial that had been found on the property during the restoration. The sundial, which is still part of the society's collections today, dates to the eighteenth century and is believed to be a commemorative piece from the Battle of Bushy Run of 1763. The sundial is octagonal in shape, being approximately twelve inches square and two inches in height. The front surface of the sundial features carvings including a serpent, a thistle, the lettering "Lat 40 35" and the Roman numerals for the actual clock face. The sundial was originally calibrated for the latitude markings of Fort Pitt, although the "Lat 40 35" inscribed on its surface is actually the latitude for Bushy Run Battlefield, located fifty miles east of Pittsburgh. The serpent carving represents the Sixtieth Royal American Regiment, one of the main regiments present at the battle; the thistle carving reflects the Scottish regiments present, including the Forty-second Black Watch and Seventy-seventh Highlanders.[144]

In October 1895, the society succeeded in purchasing Peter King's house facing Penn Avenue for $70 at sheriff's sale. The society decided to continue renting out the property for $10 per month to tenants as a way to bring in much-needed revenue for the Block House. It was also decided that once O'Hara Avenue was opened and Fort Street closed, the house would be demolished to allow for the Penn Avenue entrance to the Block House property. The home used by Matthew Golden on the other side of the property was found in heavy disrepair by June 1896. The ladies were faced with the decision of either demolishing the Golden home and allowing the

Earliest known image of the Fort Pitt sundial. The eighteenth-century stone sundial was found on the Block House property during the restoration of 1894. It commemorates the Battle of Bushy Run of 1763, which ended the Siege of Fort Pitt. *Courtesy of the Fort Pitt Society Collections.*

family to occupy the Penn Avenue house or paying for the Golden home to be repaired and continue collecting revenue off the Penn Avenue property. They opted for the latter, spending $100 in repairing the dilapidated Golden house so that they could continue to rent the other structure.[145]

The ladies wanted to make their property into a small park. They planned for a fence to extend around their property, with a formal gated entrance for visitors. The fence was a constant issue for the Fort Pitt Society because of the delay in opening O'Hara Avenue. The society felt that it could not construct a permanent fence until Fort Street was closed and O'Hara Avenue opened. By May 1900, the ladies had begun petitioning the City of Pittsburgh to vacate Point Alley so that they could proceed with constructing a brick wall around their property. Less than a month later, the women learned that the alley would not be vacated until the leases of the tenants expired. These leases would not expire for several years, and the tenants were certainly not ready to leave their homes. The costs and damages for evicting the tenants would be too much for the society to bear, and Schenley was not willing to foot the bill. Acting on the advice of their lawyer, the ladies decided to wait for the opening of O'Hara Avenue; in the meantime, a wooden fence was constructed around most of the DAR property.[146]

The finishing touches on the fence were the installation of a wrought-iron gate with the official insignia of Daughters of the American Revolution placed above the gated entrance. The gate and insignia remain today on the Block House property, having been moved at least five times since their original placement. The gate is an interesting story in that it came from the Sixth Street Suspension Bridge in Pittsburgh. Donated to the Fort Pitt Society, the gate was part of a bridge that had been designed and built by John A. Roebling in 1859, the second of four bridges that would span from Sixth Street in Downtown Pittsburgh over to Allegheny City (present-day North Shore area). The bridge was torn down in 1892 to make way for a new bridge. It is not clear from meeting minutes as to how this gate came into the possession of its donor, Ella G. Maloney, but she gave it to the ladies as early as 1898. The DAR insignia was placed over top of this gate.[147]

THE CLOSING OF FORT STREET

The fence issue happened to be the tip of the iceberg for the struggle of the DAR to maintain its property. By early December 1901, the ladies had received troubling news that O'Hara Avenue would not be opened as planned. While this was surprising to the Fort Pitt Society, what came next was even more shocking: Fort Street and Point Alley were to be officially closed! It is true that the women had actually anticipated the closing of Fort Street. One of the souvenirs they sold from the Block House was a small book entitled *Fort Duquesne and Fort Pitt*, a brief history on the French and British forts at the Point and the Block House. The book was written and published by the Fort Pitt Society. The following statement could be found inside every copy:

By 1900, the Block House property had taken on a park-like appearance, thanks to the efforts of the Fort Pitt Society. The tenement district surrounding it remained for another two years until the Pennsylvania Railroad purchased the Point. *Courtesy of the Fort Pitt Society Collections.*

> *An ordinance to close Fort Street passed the City Councils some years ago, but it was never enforced. As soon as that ordinance is carried into effect, the line of the Block House property will be extended to the middle of the street, when the passageway to Penn Avenue will be opened, and a substantial fence take the place of the temporary one at present on the ground.*[148]

The reason why the Fort Pitt Society was so approving of the plan to close Fort Street was simply because it assumed O'Hara Avenue would be opened soon after. As long as there was an entrance to the Block House property, the women were not concerned with which streets would be closed and which would remain open. If Fort Street was closed and O'Hara Avenue scrapped, the society would be forced to tear down the tenement fronting Penn Avenue so that the area could be used as a new entrance to the Block House site. Tearing down this tenement house meant a loss of up to twenty-two dollars per month for the society, funding that went directly to the Block House.[149]

To make matters worse, the entity behind the closing of Fort Street and the abandonment of O'Hara Avenue was a so-called warehouse syndicate that had plans to build several industrial warehouses at the Point. There were rumors that the syndicate would eventually turn the Point District over to railroad companies. The syndicate had placed an option on the property of the Point that was still owned by Mary Schenley (the Block House site being excluded due to its ownership by the DAR). The Fort Pitt Society's lawyer, J. Harvey White, suggested that the ladies ask for compensation and damages since they would most likely have to forfeit some of their property to the syndicate. White came up with the following plan: give the syndicate twenty feet of the original property facing O'Hara Avenue so that twenty-four feet remained between the Block House and the proposed rail lines. Damages for loss of property on both O'Hara Avenue and Fort Street were estimated at $32,750. In exchange for these damages, White suggested that the ladies ask the syndicate for an extension of sixty-five feet on Penn Avenue.[150]

The society demanded that the representative of the syndicate come to one of its meetings to discuss the official plans of the syndicate, as well as the damages to the society's property holding. The representative was Franklin F. Nicola, a well-known real estate developer in the city of Pittsburgh. Nicola had a long history with the Schenley estate, as he was behind the development of the Schenley Farms District in Oakland. The eventual results of Nicola's development of Schenley Farms included the construction of the main campus of the University of Pittsburgh, Forbes Field (former home of the Pittsburgh Pirates baseball team), Soldiers & Sailors Memorial Hall and Phipps Conservatory.[151] While not everyone agreed that a park should be built at the Point, most agreed that the Point's value was being wasted as a run-down tenement district. Nicola and the other members of the syndicate saw the potential of the Point as a terminus for railroad companies—as an area where they could build warehouses and freight stations.

Nicola attended a Fort Pitt Society meeting on December 13, 1901, during which he informed the ladies of the syndicate's intentions. His proposal was for the society to tear down its rental house on Penn Avenue, whereupon the syndicate would give an extra ten feet of property on Penn Avenue so that a proper walkway to the Block House could be constructed. He also suggested that the society build a new house somewhere on the grounds of the Block House property for the caretaker so that Golden's house could be demolished to make way for the railroad buildings. Finally, he offered $10,000 in damages. In exchange for all of this, the syndicate wanted the society to forfeit thirty-nine feet of its property facing the now abandoned

O'Hara Avenue, as well as sections of its property on Fort Street and Point Alley. This would leave only eight feet between the Block House and the proposed railroad construction instead of twenty-four feet as suggested by White. The ladies were greatly upset with this proposal and decided to discuss the matter further before making any agreements with the syndicate.[152]

AN OFFER OF REMOVAL

Negotiations between the Fort Pitt Society and the warehouse syndicate quickly began to heat up as December progressed. After attending the meeting on December 13, Nicola sent a letter to the society's attorney. The letter presented an offer to the Fort Pitt Society to have the Block House removed from the Point for a large sum of money:

> *I hereby agree to pay to the Daughters of the American Revolution…the sum of $25,000 in cash on condition that they relinquish all right, title and interest in the property now occupied by the Old Block House. In addition to this sum…I agree to remove from its present location—the Old Block House—to such location in Schenley Park as the D.A.R. elect. When removed the Block House will be put upon a satisfactory foundation; an iron fence with stone posts will be placed about the Block House, all of which work shall be under the supervision and subject to the approval of the D.A.R. and without expense to them. Further, I will agree that a tablet shall be erected on Penn Avenue on the present property of the D.A.R., without expense to them, which tablet shall be a memorial of the Fort and shall be arranged according to their instructions.*[153]

This letter is fascinating in that it blatantly proposes for the removal of the Block House to a completely different location. Schenley Park was a brand-new park built by the City of Pittsburgh in its East End section. It was named after Mary Schenley since it was she who donated much of the land that made up the park. While it would have been great to have the Block House in a nice recreational area, that area was nowhere near the Point. The historical connections between the Block House and the Point would have immediately been lost. Despite the large amount of money offered and the promise of protection of the Block House, the Fort Pitt Society was aghast at such an offer and promptly turned it down.

Word quickly spread through Pittsburgh society that the DAR had turned down the $25,000 offer to remove the Block House. Many papers claimed that the offer had been made by Mary Schenley herself and not Nicola and the syndicate. Matilda Denny instantly made a public statement in the newspapers, insisting that neither Schenley nor her agents had made such an offer. It is interesting and ironic that the ladies of the Fort Pitt Society were so quick to defend Mary Schenley despite the fact that she was the one who had given Nicola and the syndicate an option on the Point property to begin with. Perhaps they did this out of respect for Schenley—after all, she was related to most of the women. They may have even assumed that Schenley had no idea of such an offer or of Nicola's intentions. Most of all, the ladies probably realized the power (or power as they saw it) that Schenley held with her reversionary clause in the Block House deed. If they offended her in any way, she might take the Block House away from the society! In any case, Denny reassured the citizens of Pittsburgh that the Fort Pitt Society was not afraid of Nicola and his syndicate, stating in a local newspaper, "We have been told that when the syndicate begins to drive piles all around the Block House that historic little structure will undoubtedly be wrecked. That is scarcely possible, and it does not frighten us to be told such things."[154]

Nicola's offer refused, the ladies agreed to meet with him once again on December 19. This time, the recorder of the City of Pittsburgh, Joseph O. Brown, was also present, along with the attorneys of the Fort Pitt Society.[155] At the meeting, Nicola read the contents of an incriminating letter sent by the society's president, Matilda Denny, to Schenley's estate agent, William A. Herron. The exact contents of this letter remain unknown, but according to meeting minutes, Denny stated in the letter that she supported the closing of Fort Street. This letter was not sent to Herron on behalf of the society but as a personal correspondence between Denny and Herron. Still, Nicola used the letter as evidence that not all of the members of the Fort Pitt Society were against the actions taking place in the Point. He also claimed that many members supported the outright removal of the Block House. He was not the only person with this claim. A news article published the day before the meeting featured an interview of the new director of public works for Pittsburgh, J. Guy McCandless, in which he also claimed that many DAR women were supportive of moving the Block House to a new location.[156]

It is unknown which women in the Fort Pitt Society voiced their support of removal—if such women ever truly existed. Their support,

Political cartoon depicting Pittsburgh director of public works J. Guy McCandless, ordering for the removal of the Block House. The "warehouse syndicate" stands slyly behind him as the women of the Daughters of the American Revolution tremble beside the Block House. *Courtesy of the Fort Pitt Society Collections.*

however, should not be automatically condemned, especially by people of today. It is important to remember the conditions in which the Block House found itself surrounded in 1901. Standing in the middle of a place deemed by many as undesirable, the Block House would soon be overcome by towering warehouses and loud freight engines. Was a rail yard a suitable place for a historic structure? How could it possibly be preserved under such circumstances? Why not move it to a park, where it could be enjoyed by the community at large? These objections certainly made sense for the time, and yet there was a large faction in the Fort Pitt Society that strongly believed in keeping the Block House in its original location despite the odds. It was this faction that ultimately took hold of the society's leadership.

A PRIVATE MEETING

As a final effort to strike a deal with the DAR, Nicola requested a private meeting with the following society members: Matilda Wilkins Denny, Mary Elliott McCandless, Josephine Alden McConway, Anne McDowell Price Childs and Rachel Larimer Mellon. All five women were then serving on the board of directors for the Fort Pitt Society and the Advisory Committee for the society, as officers for the Pittsburgh Chapter DAR and/or on the Pittsburgh Chapter DAR Board of Management. In other words, these were women who had some power and prestige within the Fort Pitt Society and Pittsburgh Chapter DAR. Aside from this, why would Nicola specifically choose these five women?

Matilda Denny was then serving as the president of the Fort Pitt Society. She had served as regent of the Pittsburgh Chapter prior to this post and was therefore seen as an important and prestigious member of the organization as a whole (she was actually one of the first members, her name being signed on the chapter's charter). Despite her background, Denny's letter to Herron most likely made her seem sympathetic to Nicola's cause of removing the Block House. This proved to be far from the truth; she eventually became one of the loudest supporters of keeping the building in the Point.[157]

Mary Elliott McCandless was another early member of the Pittsburgh Chapter, and she was held in high esteem by her peers. She came from a very prominent family in Pittsburgh, being the daughter of locally renowned Judge Wilson McCandless and his wife, Sarah North Collins McCandless. Judge McCandless had served as United States District Court judge in the Western District of Pennsylvania from 1859 to 1876. Mary's brother, Stephen C. McCandless, was also well known throughout the Pittsburgh community, having served as a clerk of the U.S. District Court, a United States commissioner and as vice-president and treasurer of the Dollar Savings Bank in Pittsburgh. Her respect in the community alone probably prompted Nicola to request her presence at the meeting.[158]

Josephine Alden McConway was another interesting selection. Her husband was William McConway, owner of the McConway & Torley Company. The company produced Janney couplers, an essential piece of the locomotive train. His sympathies for railroad development at the Point would have been clear. He was also listed in newspapers of the time as being supportive of moving the Block House to Schenley Park, where it would be safe from destruction. Nicola most likely assumed that Josephine would follow her husband's opinion.

The fourth woman, Anne McDowell Price Childs, was also prominent in the community, as well as within the Fort Pitt Society. Her husband, Albert H. Childs, made his wealth in the iron industry and served on the boards for various financial institutions and hospitals throughout Pittsburgh.[159]

Perhaps the most interesting of the five women was Rachel Larimer Mellon, a member of the prestigious Mellon family of Pittsburgh. At the time of Nicola's proposed meeting, Rachel was serving as the vice-president general for the National Society of the Daughters of the American Revolution, as well as serving various roles in the Pittsburgh Chapter. Rachel's husband, James Ross Mellon, was the son of Judge Thomas Mellon. Judge Mellon founded T. Mellon & Sons, the bank that eventually became the world-renowned Mellon Financial Corporation (currently the Bank of New York Mellon). One of Rachel's brothers-in-law was Andrew Mellon, the longest-serving U.S. treasurer in United States history and one of the wealthiest men in the world in 1901. Her son, William Larimer Mellon Sr., was also prominent, later playing a key role in the Gulf Oil Company. Rachel's father, William Larimer, was himself a major railroad baron and landowner. Larimer was the president of the Pittsburgh & Connellsville Railroad, one of the first railroads in western Pennsylvania and later accumulated by the Baltimore & Ohio Railroad, a subsidy of the Pennsylvania Railroad. Larimer eventually moved to the western United States, where he served various political positions and helped found the city of Denver, Colorado. All of her connections considered, it makes perfect sense as to why Nicola would want Rachel Larimer Mellon to be part of his special meeting.[160]

Amazingly, all five women refused to meet with Nicola. Although they had strong social standings and the opinions of their menfolk often against them, the women remained steadfast in their belief that the Block House should stay in its original location. The claims of Nicola and others that the DAR was supportive of Block House removal were beginning to wear thin. Initially appearing to be divided in opinion, by early 1902, a united front had begun to take form among the Fort Pitt Society. This unity was brought about by the regent of the Pittsburgh Chapter DAR, Edith Darlington Ammon.

EDITH TAKES COMMAND

To call Edith Dennison Darlington Ammon the champion of the Fort Pitt Block House would be a more than appropriate description. Ammon spent most of her adult life working toward the preservation of the little building, determined that it would not be removed or torn down. Edith was born just outside Pittsburgh in 1862 on her family's estate. Her father, William McCullough Darlington, was a well-respected and wealthy lawyer who married Mary Carson O'Hara, granddaughter of James O'Hara and first cousin to Mary Elizabeth Croghan Schenley. Mary inherited her grandfather's country estate, Guyasuta, situated outside Pittsburgh along the Allegheny River (present-day locations of Sharpsburg and O'Hara Township).[161] This estate became the primary home of the Darlington family. Edith had two older siblings who survived to adulthood—a brother, O'Hara Darlington, and a sister, Mary O'Hara Darlington.[162]

William and Mary Darlington both instilled in their children a passion for history, particularly western Pennsylvania history. Mr. Darlington had a large collection of early manuscripts and maps of Pittsburgh, and Mrs. Darlington wrote many publications on the history of Fort Pitt and the colonial era of Pittsburgh. (Today, the Darlingtons' collections make up the bulk of the Darlington Memorial Library at the University of Pittsburgh.[163]) Edith and her sister, Mary, joined the Pittsburgh Chapter shortly after it was formed in 1891. Around the same time, Edith married Pittsburgh lawyer Samuel A. Ammon. The new Mrs. Ammon quickly worked her way up into the ranks of the Pittsburgh Chapter, being named regent of the chapter in 1899. She would hold this post for the next ten years.[164]

At the time Edith Ammon became regent, the closing of Fort Street and abandoning of O'Hara Avenue had not yet been announced. Her first two years in office were relatively calm, with most of her efforts focusing on the chapter and not necessarily the Block House. Her love for the Block House, however, became evident as the controversy with Nicola and the warehouse syndicate began to swell. She was greatly disturbed by the claims published in

Portrait of Edith Darlington Ammon on her wedding day. Ammon was a leading member of the Pittsburgh Chapter NSDAR and Fort Pitt Society for many years. She worked hard to save the Block House from destruction by the Pennsylvania Railroad. *Courtesy of the Fort Pitt Society Collections.*

newspapers that the Daughters of the American Revolution were supportive of the removal of the Block House. Using her rank as regent, she moved forward to put an end to these rumors and to assist the Fort Pitt Society Board of Directors in the fight to save the Block House.

THE RAILROAD'S PLANS

It was in early January 1902 when the rumors of railroad involvement at the Point came closer to the truth. An exposé published in the *Pittsburgh Leader* revealed that the Pennsylvania Railroad, one of the most powerful railroad corporations of its time, did indeed have plans for expanding its property to the Point District. The railroad's tracks would be extended down to the Point by either an extension of already existing lines on Liberty Avenue or by constructing an elevated track on Duquesne Way. The exposé also suggested that the reason for the Pennsylvania Railroad's plans was to beat out competition from another company, the Wabash Railroad. Despite newspaper claims of the warehouse syndicate working hand in hand with the Pennsylvania Railroad, the syndicate strongly denied any plans to sell the Point District to any railroad corporation.[165]

Other newspapers were also reporting on the plans, especially concerning the construction of the elevated tracks on Duquesne Way. The surface tracks on Liberty Avenue were unpopular since they cut through the heart of the downtown business district of the city. If the railroad chose the Liberty Avenue plan, the surface tracks would not only remain, but they would also extend the entire length down to the lower areas of the Point. The Pennsylvania Railroad already had a freight depot on the outer edge of the Point District called the Duquesne Freight Depot. Built in 1854, it was located within the area of the site of Fort Pitt, not too far from the Block House. Reports claimed that the railroad would construct a newer freight depot in the heart of the Point, as well as connections to rail lines such as the Baltimore & Ohio Railroad, the Pittsburgh & Western Railroad and the Fort Wayne Railroad (all subsidies of the Pennsylvania Railroad). The Pennsylvania's rival, the Wabash, had recently constructed a passenger terminal near the Point at Ferry and Liberty Streets. By acquiring the Point property and building connections for its own rail lines, the Pennsylvania could effectively cut off the Wabash's access to the Allegheny River, making it difficult for the railroad to connect to its passenger terminal. Purchasing

Another political cartoon highlighting the legal battles between the Daughters of the American Revolution, the Pittsburgh Chamber of Commerce and the Pittsburgh Coal Exchange against the warehouse syndicate. Many citizens and businessmen were concerned about the fate of the Point should the syndicate or railroad take over the district. *Courtesy of the Fort Pitt Society Collections.*

the Point was not just a way for the Pennsylvania Railroad to extends its lines and build its warehouses; it was a way to force out the competition.[166]

As the railroad's plans became clearer, the ladies grew more concerned, especially Edith Ammon. Although the warehouse syndicate consistently denied any involvement with the railroad, it was obvious to Ammon and others that the ultimate plan for the Point was industrialization and redevelopment. That plan would happen quickly if the Fort Pitt Society did not attempt to stop it. Ammon found herself faced with two major tasks—first, to stop the warehouse syndicate from taking over the Point, and second, to turn the Point into a park so that its history could be preserved.

THE FIRST STEPS

Ammon's first step was to tackle the accusations against the DAR from Nicola and the syndicate. Frustrated by his failed attempts to remove the Block House, Frank Nicola began to publicly accuse the Fort Pitt Society of supporting the removal of the historic structure and the closing of Fort Street. Charges of this nature were already featured in the papers before, but starting in early 1902, Nicola went full force in accusing the DAR of initially being supportive of the changes at the Point. He had documents to prove his argument, such as the infamous December 1901 letter written by Matilda Denny and the paragraph in the society's Fort Pitt booklet in which it was specifically stated that the DAR looked forward to the closing of Fort Street. Ammon released an official statement from the Fort Pitt Society that addressed the accusations. She completely agreed with Nicola that Denny had, in fact, supported the closing of Fort Street, but only because there was still another access point to the Block House from Penn Avenue. She did not support the redevelopment of the Point District into a rail yard. Secondly, the opinion Denny provided in the letter was not the official opinion of the Fort Pitt Society. The letter was a private correspondence between Denny and Herron; it was not meant to be used as an official statement of the organization. Finally, Ammon defended the booklet and its incriminating passage by simply stating that it was just a book and not a legal argument. Despite her defense of the booklet, all future copies omitted the passage so as to avoid further controversy.[167]

Ammon and the other ladies had to deal with other charges, such as Director of Public Works J. Guy McCandless's claim that the Block House did not receive enough visitors to necessitate it remaining in the Point. Numerous articles were published by the Fort Pitt Society, often anonymously, providing statistics and other information on visitation at the Block House so as to dispel these claims. The ladies also reached out for support from other organizations, such as the Sons of the American Revolution, the Pittsburgh Chamber of Commerce and the Pennsylvania Society of Colonial Dames of America. The Colonial Dames was an important one since the president of the Pennsylvania Society was the wife of A.J. Cassatt, the president of the Pennsylvania Railroad. To have the approval and support of Mrs. Cassatt would clearly be beneficial to the ladies and their cause. The women also appealed to the wife of Senator William Flinn, a powerful politician from Pittsburgh. It was published in the papers of the time that Rachel Larimer Mellon had encouraged Mrs. Flinn to visit the Block House and to take part in the protest against the warehouse syndicate. While it was never stated whether Mrs. Flinn actually visited the building, it was mentioned that she strongly opposed the removal of the Block House.[168]

As the ladies garnered support for their cause, Ammon moved on to investigating the warehouse syndicate and its dealings with the Schenley estate. She discovered that a petition had been signed and given to city councils requesting the vacation of Fort Street and Point Alley. It was from this petition that the ordinance was passed to close the streets. The signatures on the petition were none other than those of Franklin Nicola and John W. Herron, the son and business partner of William Herron. This was an outrage to Ammon since Nicola did not own any property at the Point (he only had an option on portions of the property—this would expire on April 1, 1902). In order for the petition to be valid, the majority owner(s) of the Point had to sign it—this would be Mary Schenley. Schenley, of course, had reserved all property rights to the Block House property in regard to the opening and closing streets at the Point. Although Herron was Schenley's power of attorney, Ammon argued that his legal duties as laid out by Schenley did not provide him outright permission to sign petitions in relation to the property. At a meeting held on February 13, 1902, Ammon and the ladies of the Fort Pitt Society decided to file suit against the petition.[169]

A PARK FOR THE POINT

Around the same time as this decision, it was also decided to file a petition with the city council's Finance Committee for funding to construct a "Point Park" around the Block House. The petition featured 150 signatures of property owners and citizens from Pittsburgh. According to one of the directors of the Fort Pitt Society, Mary Kingsley Clarke, the petition for the park

> *was not made with the sole object of protecting* [the Block House] *property. It was also made in behalf of the many who have so little of pleasure and sunshine in their lives. The "Point" is a spot for which nature has done much; man nothing...*[Other cities] *are erecting monuments to commemorate the brave deeds done there. We have a monument in that scarred, weather-beaten old "Block House," more inspiring than the most significant pile of granite could be, and which commemorates deeds as brave as ever stood recorded. If anything is to be done to save the "Block*

> *House" and to beautify that part of the city, it must be done now. We are working for the past, the present, and time to come.*[170]

The Finance Committee suggested that the ladies ask Mary Schenley to give the property herself, but the DAR turned this down due to lack of time. The committee refused to pay for "Point Park" out of the city's park appropriations; it also went against the women's plea that the park could serve as an annex to Schenley Park in Oakland. The society's arguments of the historical significance of the Point and the need for more parks in the city finally convinced the committee to look into the matter further. Although filed on February 14, 1902, the committee did not pass the petition on to city councils until March 29.[171]

The effort to create a city park at the Point became more and more difficult. Since 1836, there had been discussions both serious in nature and poetic to have some sort of park at the Point to commemorate its history. Was it now the time for such a park to be constructed? The Finance Committee had passed on the petition for the park to the city councils, but it became bogged down in debates among the council members. Nicola and the warehouse syndicate were also turning public opinion against the park since it would cost citizen tax dollars for such a venture by the city. Was the Point really a place for a park? The idea of progress over sentiment was widely promoted by industrialists and politicians alike at this time. Any railroad or warehouse construction at the Point would be "improvements" to the property, not hindrances. As the railroad plan for the Point came closer to reality, citizens became worried about the proposed improvements. Will they benefit the city? What will happen to the Block House? What about the Pittsburgh Exposition buildings along the Allegheny River?[172] Will the construction of railroad property block river traffic along the Monongahela Wharf? What will happen to the Wabash Railroad? These were some of the many questions posed to political and business leaders in the city as the people of Pittsburgh wondered whether or not the construction of the warehouses at the Point was really "progress."

As councils moved further away from the park petition, Edith Ammon decided to appeal to the city's chamber of commerce. The chamber turned down the park idea in April 1902, but it decided to hear a plea from Edith Ammon in June. The plea worked to a certain extent in that the chamber was unanimous that the Block House should not be moved from the Point; however, it did not approve for a park in the Point to help with the preservation of the Block House. The decision of the chamber to reject the idea of a

The Fort Pitt Society's hopes for a park at the Point were crushed when the Pittsburgh Chamber of Commerce ultimately rejected the proposal for such a park. It seemed as though the Daughters of the American Revolution were now deserted. *Courtesy of the Fort Pitt Society Collections.*

"Point Park" was not easily resolved. Members argued with one another over the issue, with one gentleman stating that providing a park for the area around the Block House was an act of patriotism, not sentimentalism. Turning the Point into an industrial center was "placing commercialism and greed above all ideas of patriotism." Another member countered this argument by stating that it was "commercialism, not sentiment, that had made Pittsburgh." The chamber ultimately recommended that the Fort Pitt Society purchase additional property through private funding so that the Penn Avenue entrance could be widened to one hundred feet; this proposal was rejected by the society.[173]

The "Point Park" idea was quickly losing support, and the DAR realized that its efforts now rested solely with saving the Block House from removal and/or destruction.

THE BATTLE BEGINS

The Fort Pitt Society filed a petition on February 15, 1902, with the Court of Common Pleas of Allegheny County, asking for the ordinances closing Fort Street and Point Alley to be declared null and void. The basis of their argument was that the petition for the ordinances had not been signed by the legal owners of the Point. On this same day, they also filed a bill in equity with the court. The suit was specifically filed against Frank Nicola, John W. Herron, the City of Pittsburgh and Mary Schenley. It is interesting to note that despite naming Schenley in the proceedings, the Fort Pitt Society never spoke out against her or accused her publicly for the closing of Fort Street and Point Alley.[174] A demurrer was instantly filed against the DAR's suit, claiming that without property rights the ladies were not the official owners of the Block House. Therefore, they had no right to file any suit regarding the ordinances. This demurrer was heard in court on March 8, 1902, where it was overruled. The society's suit was finally argued in court in June, with a decision being reached by the twenty-first. The court ultimately ruled in favor of the Fort Pitt Society by declaring the ordinances null and void. It seemed the Daughters of the American Revolution had won its battle, but it had only just begun the fight.

The court's decision was appealed by Schenley, Nicola, Herron and the city all the way to the Supreme Court of Pennsylvania. The appeal was heard by the court in November 1902, whereupon the decision of the lower court was overturned. The Supreme Court ruled that Herron legally signed the petition for the ordinances as power of attorney for Schenley. Although it was not specifically stated in Herron's contract with Schenley, the court felt that it implied he had the legal right to petition in her name.[175] It was also difficult for the court to find sympathy with the Fort Pitt Society since it had essentially given away its property rights (including the right to petition on behalf of the property) when the society signed the deed to the Block House eight years earlier.

This decision was not the only setback the Fort Pitt Society faced by the end of 1902. Rumors circulated throughout Pittsburgh that Henry Clay Frick, an infamous and powerful Pittsburgh industrialist, had purchased the Point District from Mary Schenley for millions of dollars. These rumors began in early 1902 and continued to grow as the year passed on. Frick consistently denied any claims that he had purchased the Point or even that he had plans to purchase the property. It was well known that Frick was against the "Point Park" idea and supported industrial development at the

Point. His thoughts on the issue were published in newspapers at the time, with him stating outright that while it would be best for the Block House to be kept in a park, that park should not be located in the Point. The Point should be used for "commercial improvements."[176] Despite all of his denials, it was revealed in October 1902 that Frick had, in fact, purchased all of the Schenley property at the Point as early as February for a whopping $2 million! Not only had he purchased the property from Schenley, but he had also purchased the reversionary clause in the Block House deed. This meant that if the Fort Pitt Society failed in its efforts to take care of the Block House, the property would revert back to Frick, not the Schenley heirs. The reversionary clause only cost him $10.[177]

The ladies of the Fort Pitt Society were stunned. It was one thing to fight off Nicola and the city but quite another thing to go up against Henry Clay Frick! It was discovered that Frick actually accumulated numerous properties at the Point aside from Mary Schenley's estate. Even more worrisome was that Frick purchased all of the properties with the intention that they would be leased or even sold outright to the Pennsylvania Railroad. One newspaper claimed that Frick planned to lease to the Pennsylvania Railroad for twenty-five years at $90,150 per year, with the option of buying the property for $3 million at the expiration of the lease. Other reports of this nature were published repeatedly by papers throughout Pittsburgh. Only a few days after the revelation of Frick's purchase, an ordinance was introduced in city councils by the railroad company. This ordinance asked for the right-of-way for an elevated track from the railroad's Union Station (located on upper Penn Avenue) to the Point District. The company also asked for approval to raise the grade of the Point along Penn Avenue below Third Street. These requests remained bogged down in councils over the next year.[178]

A BILL FOR THE BLOCK HOUSE

The year 1903 would prove to be a busy one for the Fort Pitt Society as it moved forward in its fight to save the Block House. It was in January that the society learned that its case was overturned by the Supreme Court of Pennsylvania, with no chance for further appeals. With the park plan completely out of the picture as well, the ladies had to find a different approach to their dilemma. Ideas were tossed around, including asking Frick for additional property on their Penn Avenue frontage. The idea that had

The Fort Pitt Society of the Daughters of the American Revolution achieved victory in June 1902 after winning a court battle against the warehouse syndicate. Unfortunately, this victory was short-lived: the Supreme Court of Pennsylvania overturned the lower court decision in October 1902. *Courtesy of the Fort Pitt Society Collections.*

the most support was one proposed by Edith Ammon: introducing a bill into Pennsylvania legislature that would save the Block House from destruction and/or removal by Frick and the railroad.

The plan for a bill protecting the Block House and other historical structures from eminent domain by the railroad was a relatively good plan since Pennsylvania had just elected a new governor who not only supported the preservation of historic structures but also felt it was the duty of the state to assist with this preservation. The governor was Samuel W. Pennypacker. He was strongly against eminent domain as practiced by railroads and other corporations. This stance further suited the Fort Pitt Society's efforts against the Pennsylvania Railroad and Frick.[179]

Edith Ammon worked on drafting the bill with assistance from her husband, Samuel, and his law partners, Edward B. Scull and A.M. Imbrie. The bill was passed through the state House of Representatives in early February, with its introduction into the state Senate by Senator John Goehring on February 19, 1903. It was in the Senate where the proposed legislation began to flounder, mainly caused by the introduction of another bill. This other bill was presented by Senator John C. Grady, and it extended the rights of the railroads, especially eminent domain. The last thing Edith Ammon and the other ladies wanted was a law that gave even more powers to the railroad—this would only make it easier for it to remove the Block House.[180]

Although the Fort Pitt Society found support from Pennypacker, it had a difficult time finding support in the Senate. Many senators relied heavily on votes and campaign funding from railroad barons and other industrialists. To play against them by voting for the Ammon bill could be a costly mistake. Edith Ammon decided to lobby for the bill herself and spent most of March in Harrisburg promoting the proposed law. Her efforts were followed closely in Pittsburgh newspapers, as well as other publications across the state. In a world where women had few rights, especially lacking the right to vote, it was amazing to see a woman lobbying the legislature and attending conferences and meetings with prestigious congressmen. The bill actually became known as the "Mrs. Ammon bill."[181]

It was soon decided to merge the Grady bill and Ammon bill into one so that both railroad supporters and preservationists could be satisfied. The new merged bill still protected historical structures, but issues such as eminent domain remained stronger than ever. Despite its support of eminent domain, Ammon continued pushing for the new bill since it ultimately protected the Block House. In one of her lobbying efforts, Edith spoke to a room full of state senators, urging their support for the bill. She gave the following quote:

> *Have you no history? Have you no pride?…Men who would allow this precious spot to be sacrificed certainly have no pride at all. If these* [historic] *sites are destroyed nothing but written pages will be left behind to tell of their memory. Future generations will want to see them. We should not deny them the opportunity.*[182]

By mid-April, the bill had passed both the House of Representatives and the Senate; it now awaited approval by Governor Pennypacker. Letters of petition were sent by schoolchildren in Pittsburgh, pleading with Pennypacker to save the Block House by passing the bill into law. Despite the lobbying efforts of Ammon and others, Pennypacker ultimately vetoed the bill on April 30, 1903. Although he supported historic preservation, he still felt the bill gave too much power to the railroads. He also disliked how the bill only favored those historic structures owned by corporations or societies, such as the Block House. What about those structures that did not have the support of an organization such as the Daughters of the American Revolution?[183] The bill was not revived, and the DAR moved on.

THE BATTLE CONTINUES

It seemed as though the ladies were experiencing nothing but failure. The park petition was rejected. Their court case against the closing of Fort Street and Point Alley was overturned. Their bill to save the Block House was vetoed. The attempt to purchase extra land from Frick also failed—and for an alarming reason. Frick simply told the women that he could not sell any land at the Point because he no longer owned the property. The property had finally been sold to the Pennsylvania Railroad.[184]

What was the next step for the Fort Pitt Society? Remarkably, the women continued on in their crusade to save the building they treasured. With the sale of the Point to the railroad and the streets formally closed, the Fort Pitt Society received an official notice from the City of Pittsburgh awarding the organization $1,000 in damages for the closing of Fort Street. While this may have seemed a victory for the ladies, Ammon and her colleagues were outraged. They received nothing for the closing of Point Alley, a closure that also affected their property and its value. Furthermore, the closing of both Fort Street and Point Alley would force the women to tear down their remaining rental property on Penn Avenue

An image of early Pittsburgh Chapter NSDAR/Fort Pitt Society women, including Edith Darlington Ammon (front, second from left) and Rachel Larimer Mellon (front, second from right). *Courtesy of the Fort Pitt Society Collections.*

so that the area could be used as a new access point for the Block House site. This removal would cost them much-needed revenue for maintaining their property. A suit was filed in the summer of 1903 by the Fort Pitt

Society against the City of Pittsburgh. The women demanded $50,000 in damages for the closing of both streets.[185]

It was very difficult for the Fort Pitt Society to gain sympathy from the city and others when it came to the damage claims. The Penn Avenue frontage was specifically given to the ladies by Schenley so that it could be used as an access point when Fort Street and Point Alley closed. The women knew full well about this intention, too, as evidenced by letters written to Herron & Sons and in their published booklet, *Fort Duquesne and Fort Pitt*, where it was openly stated that they expected the streets to be closed so that the Penn Avenue entrance could be opened. This evidence was used extensively in their case against the ordinances in 1902—a case they ultimately failed to win. While it is obvious that the DAR initially supported the street closures, it is not as clear as to whether or not it completely understood the purpose behind the closures. Had Bigelow led them to believe that the Point would eventually become a park, hence why the streets had to be closed off? Did they feel at the time in 1894 that any "commercial improvements" at the Point would have no effect on the Block House? Perhaps the women even assumed that the street closings would never happen—after all, nearly ten years had passed between the proposal to close the streets and the actual closing of the streets.

While waiting for their damage suit to make it to court, the ladies moved on to dealing with the Pennsylvania Railroad. The ordinance providing the railroad with the right-of-way, as well as giving it permission to raise the grade level at the Point, was finally passed in March 1904. This ordinance obviously angered the women since it meant that without a doubt the railroad would be moving into the Point. It was also frustrating because raising the grade level of the Point presented the Fort Pitt Society with a major problem. If the grade level were raised, the Block House would almost have to be lifted up to the higher level. The only other option was to keep the building where it stood, with high retaining walls around the property. This would save the building from being moved from its original foundations, but it would be hard for people to see the structure since it would be sitting down in a lower area surrounded by high walls. It was ultimately decided to keep the building in its exact original location, with high fencing and walls built around it to protect it from the rail yard.[186]

A Home for the Caretaker

On July 27, 1904, the Fort Pitt Society filed yet another lawsuit, asking the courts to stop the Pennsylvania Railroad from damaging its property, particularly the sections to the north of the Block House building. The women decided to hire Edith Ammon's husband, Samuel, and his law firm to represent them full time on all of their legal battles. Edith and Samuel began to work hard on

This photograph depicts the construction of the Pennsylvania Railroad's new buildings at the Point. The Fort Pitt Society's caretaker's lodge is visible on the right side of the image, with the Block House sitting directly behind it (underneath the American flag). The ground level had already been increased for the railroad, hence why the Block House appears "sunken" into the ground. *Courtesy of the Thomas & Katherine Detre Library and Archives, Sen. John Heinz History Center.*

gathering evidence and other important documents for their case against the Pennsylvania Railroad. They had to act fast because as early as October 1904, the railroad began to demolish the tenement houses and other structures at the Point to make way for its warehouses and tracks.

At the same time that the demolition began, the society's damage suit finally made it to court, with hearings starting in late October 1904. Amazingly, the women were awarded $18,300 in damages; however, the city instantly appealed this decision. The damage suit and its appeals continued for another eight months. Meanwhile, Edith spent most of her free time at the site of Block House, making sure that no harm came to the historic structure from the demolition going on around it. Wrecking balls, dynamite and burning debris all threatened the safety of the Block House, and there was little that Edith and the women could do about it.

Another troubling issue was the Golden home. Matthew Golden's house was extremely weakened by the removal of an adjoining house during

In order to keep constant surveillance over the Block House property, the Fort Pitt Society constructed the caretaker's lodge in 1905 so that the Block House caretaker could live on-site. The Block House itself is peeking out from behind the lodge in the right side of this photograph. *Courtesy of the Archives Service Center, University of Pittsburgh.*

railroad demolition. (That house sat on railroad property, while Golden's house straddled Fort Pitt Society and railroad property.) Matthew had recently passed away, but the society hired his wife, Mary, to be the new caretaker. Mary and her children needed a new home since their old house was in desperate need of repair. The ladies were faced with the decision to build a new home for their caretaker. The best place to build such a structure was on their Penn Avenue frontage—the same location in which their other rental property stood. They initially discussed having Mary Golden move into the rental property, but it was also in need of repair work. The Fort Pitt Society had reached a dead end: its Penn Avenue frontage would have to be cleared out for a new home for its caretaker.[187]

The "caretaker's lodge," as the building came to be known, stood in front of the Block House's western wall where the main entrance to the building was located. The wrought-iron gates given to the society in 1898 were moved in front of the house, with a walkway leading back behind to the Block House. With the high fences and walls surrounding the Block House and the caretaker's lodge out in front, it almost appeared as if the Block House was sunken into someone's backyard! The caretaker's lodge was completed and opened on October 5, 1905. The building served as both a house for the Block House caretaker and as space for meetings and events for the Fort Pitt Society. The house remained in use until 1966, when it was demolished as part of the construction of Point State Park.[188]

A LAW IS PASSED

The Fort Pitt Society's damage lawsuit finally came to an end in May 1905. Although initially awarded more than $18,000 in damages by the courts, the decision was appealed by the City of Pittsburgh. After a series of hearings, the court finally offered the women $12,000 total in damages. The ladies were advised by Samuel Ammon and his partners to accept the offer and move on; this advice was heeded. The amount awarded was certainly not enough to sustain the costs to maintain and improve their property, but the DAR accepted the small victory with pride.[189]

While the court battles were raging on, Edith Ammon began drafting another bill to save the Block House and other historical sites from destruction. As early as February 1905, she went to Harrisburg to meet with politicians in an effort to push for the introduction of the bill into state legislature. Michael H. Kennedy, a young state senator from Pittsburgh, agreed to introduce the bill on behalf of Edith Ammon and the Fort Pitt Society. Two years passed before Ammon and Kennedy were successful in pushing the bill through the state House of Representatives and Senate. In 1907, the governor of Pennsylvania was Edwin Stuart, also a staunch supporter of historic preservation. Stuart signed the bill into law, thereby securing the safety of the Block House from demolition by the Pennsylvania Railroad. The language of the law was mainly written by Edith Ammon herself. It read as follows:

> *Be it enacted that no corporation now incorporated under the law of this state, or which shall hereafter be incorporated thereunder, shall exercise the right of eminent domain as against the land now occupied by any building which was used during the Colonial or Revolutionary period as a place of assembly by the Council of the Colony of Pennsylvania, or by the Supreme Executive Council of the Commonwealth of Pennsylvania, or by the Congress of the United States; or as against the land now*

Photograph of Edith Ammon, probably taken in 1907 upon the passing of Pennsylvania legislation protecting the Block House and other historical structures from eminent domain by private corporations. *Courtesy of the Fort Pitt Society Collections.*

> *occupied by any fort, redoubt, or blockhouse erected during said Colonial or Revolutionary period; or as against any building used as headquarters by the Commander-in-chief of the Continental Army; or as against the site of any such building, fort, redoubt, blockhouse or headquarters, which said building, redoubt, blockhouse or headquarters, or site thereof is now or shall hereafter be preserved for its historic memories and associations, and not for private profit. Provided, That the said Colonial and Revolutionary period, as applied to the buildings, forts, redoubts, blockhouses or headquarters, or the sites thereof, as aforesaid, shall be taken as ended on the third day of September, Anno Domini one thousand seven hundred and eight-three. Approved the 10th day of May, A.D. 1907. Edwin S. Stuart.*[190]

The Fort Pitt Society celebrated its victory by hosting a special ceremony on Flag Day, 1907. Senator Kennedy was invited to the celebration whereupon he received a special gift from the ladies: a clock in a silver case inscribed with his initials and an engraving which thanked him for all of his efforts in helping to save the Block House. The Fort Pitt Society had won its fight in the state legislature—the Block House was here to stay.[191]

THE BATTLE ENDS

In June 1911, Edith Darlington Ammon gave a report to the women of the Daughters of the American Revolution of Allegheny County. Ten years had passed since the ladies first took action against Nicola and the warehouse syndicate. So much had changed during that decade. The Point, once one of the largest slum districts in the city, was now an industrialized rail yard for the Pennsylvania Railroad. Mary Schenley was gone, having passed away in 1903. A new caretaker's house for the DAR stood along Penn Avenue, one of two main thoroughfares left in the Point following the street closures. The only thing that had remained constant in those ten years was the Fort Pitt Block House. It still stood in its original spot, restored to its 1764 appearance and open for visitors to learn its history.

The court battles against the Pennsylvania Railroad began with the lawsuit filed in 1904. Those battles continued all the way to the Supreme Court of Pennsylvania, where the Fort Pitt Society ultimately failed in stopping the railroad from surrounding the Block House and taking over the Point. By January 1911, the fight was officially over; there were no further chances of appeal, and the ladies had to concede to the fact that the railroad was here to stay. Addressing her fellow chapter members, Edith said that comments regarding the case against the railroad were unnecessary, but she "had at no time been blinded by the smoke of the Pennsylvania Railroad."[192]

The Fort Pitt Society found itself defeated more than once, but its victories were impressive considering the time and place. The ladies had succeeded where so many others had failed by keeping the Block House from railroad demolition. At any time, they could have simply moved the historic building to a nearby park, thus sparing themselves of costly court battles and decade-long struggles. They went up against some powerful entities, such as the Pennsylvania Railroad and Henry Clay Frick. They lobbied state legislatures for historic preservation over eminent domain in an era that was not exceptionally known for preservation efforts or denying railroad corporations their incredible powers. The Fort Pitt Society was ahead of its time in pushing for a park at the Point, although it would

The Block House and caretaker's lodge in 1915. Railway cars and tracks rest just beyond the Block House behind the high retaining wall, and large warehouses loom in the background. The railroad's plans for the Point District were now complete. *Courtesy of the Archives Service Center, University of Pittsburgh.*

not be long before the idea of a Point State Park would come to fruition. In a time where women had few rights and much expectations of certain behavior, the ladies of the Fort Pitt Society went against the grain by fighting for what they believed was right. Edith Ammon said it best when she spoke the following words:

> *Men—with but the thought of gain and gold were dreaming of tracks and trains, of massive walls and wreathing smoke from towering chimneys, while we dreamed of fame and power, of peaceful paths where once was strife, of space and breeze, of floating flags and trees, not smoke and noise. They planned for vandalism—we for patriotism. Patriotism wins.*[193]

Chapter 4

Point State Park and the Block House Today

Just think how many stories came from the Block House!

After 1907, the Fort Pitt Society of the Daughters of the American Revolution no longer had to fear threats of Block House removal or destruction since the law was passed in state legislature prohibiting the removal of colonial and Revolutionary structures due to eminent domain. Although the ladies were successful in saving the historic structure from destruction, they were not successful in saving the rest of the Point from the clutches of the Pennsylvania Railroad. As the twentieth century progressed, the Fort Pitt Society continued in its efforts to promote, maintain and protect the Fort Pitt Block House. The Point, however, became increasingly blighted as the railroad and other property owners spent less time maintaining their properties and structures. The creation of Point State Park in the late 1950s and early 1960s led to a new era in the Point's history, as well as in the Block House's history. Today, the Fort Pitt Block House stands in the middle of one of the most beautiful urban parks in the United States.

The Early Twentieth Century

The first decade of the twentieth century was filled with legal battles for the Fort Pitt Society as it continued to fight for the Block House's survival. With

Postcard image of the Point from 1936, showing its industrial growth and the bridges that blocked it from view. It was around this time that city leaders began to seriously consider the idea of a park at the Point. *Courtesy of the Fort Pitt Society Collections.*

the passing of Edith's Law in 1907 and the official end to the court cases in 1911, the Block House entered the second decade with relatively little drama. The women of the Fort Pitt Society faced the task of encouraging people to visit the Block House despite being surrounded by ugly warehouses and loud freight engines. It was difficult for potential visitors to find the building because of its surroundings, especially since the ladies were forced to keep it standing at a much lower level than the rest of the Point so that the Block House could remain in its exact original location. Despite this, the building saw thousands of visitors every year, and the women held many patriotic events and celebrations at the Block House throughout the twentieth century.

It was during this time that a renaissance of sorts began in Pittsburgh. People were starting to take seriously the conditions of areas like the Point, realizing that urban renewal was desperately needed. In 1918, the Citizens' Committee on the City Plan for Pittsburgh was formed; the committee's name eventually changed to the Municipal Planning Association. The group was able to conduct numerous studies on Pittsburgh's parks, railways, rivers and streets, but it was unable to find a solution for the Point. One of the main issues of making the Point into a park was the presence of the bridges at the tip of the Point—the Manchester Bridge leading across the Allegheny River and the Point Bridge leading across the Monongahela River. These

Image of the Block House from circa 1945. The Point District had become one of many eyesores that city leaders wanted to improve. It was difficult to encourage people to visit the Block House due to its surroundings and due to the fact that it was barely visible beneath warehouses and retaining walls. *Courtesy of the Thomas & Katherine Detre Library and Archives, Sen. John Heinz History Center.*

bridges provided access from downtown to neighborhoods in the North Side and South Side sections of the city. In order for a proper park to be established at the Point, the bridges and their connecting roadways would have to be eliminated. Such a removal would cause major traffic congestion and concerns for Pittsburgh—an issue not worth having over a park.[194]

A National Park

Aside from traffic problems, there was also concern over who would pay for and build such a park. Financing for a park at the Point had also been a major issue back when the Fort Pitt Society was pushing for "Point Park."

Many citizens who were interested in having a park at the Point quickly lost interest when they realized what it would cost the city and its taxpayers. The onset of the Great Depression in the early 1930s temporarily ended any further discussions on the renewal of the Point. It was not until 1937 that steps were taken to approach the federal government for assistance on building a park. It was in this year that the president of the Pittsburgh Chamber of Commerce, Frank C. Harper, pushed for a resolution to create a national park at the Point commemorating George Washington. Harper was supported by the president of the Historical Society of Western Pennsylvania, John S. Fisher.[195]

The city immediately announced its support of Harper and Fisher, and the Point Park Commission was formed by the city council. A preliminary plan was created that included the allotment of thirty-six acres and a floodwall for the park, the reconstruction of Fort Duquesne and Fort Pitt,

Another view of the Point from the early twentieth century. The Block House property is the cluster of trees seen on the left side of the photo beyond the railroad tracks. The Pittsburgh Exposition Society buildings are seen on the right side of the photo. *Courtesy of the Thomas & Katherine Detre Library and Archives, Sen. John Heinz History Center.*

the construction of a museum and exposition hall and parking for about seven thousand vehicles. It was also recommended that the bridges at the tip of the Point be pushed back so as to allow more recreational space for the park and better access to the rivers.

City officials met with the National Park Service (NPS) in December 1938 to discuss the possibility of having a national park at the Point. The meeting was disappointing in that the NPS would not enter official negotiations with Pittsburgh until all of the area included in the proposed park was acquired by the city and handed over to the NPS. The age-old issue of lack of funding made it impossible for the city to acquire the park land on its own. Even if it was able to do so, there was still no guarantee from the NPS that Congress would make an appropriation for the creation of Point Park, as it was to be called. Finally, the NPS insisted that the entire Fort Pitt would have to be reconstructed exactly the way it was in the eighteenth century. This meant less room for an actual park and renaissance development.[196]

Despite the concerns presented by the NPS requirements, the city continued its negotiations over the next three years. Archaeological excavations were conducted in 1941 and 1942 to determine the original locations of Fort Pitt and Fort Duquesne; this work was largely completed by Wesley L. Bliss. Bliss's dig and resulting report were the first of their kind for the Point as no other official archaeological excavations had ever taken place previously.[197] Things seemed to be going relatively well when the bombing of Pearl Harbor occurred on December 7, 1941. The United States entered World War II, and the plans for Point Park were cast aside once again.

POINT STATE PARK

It was after the war that the Point Park idea gained new strength with support from the Pittsburgh Regional Planning Association (formerly the Municipal Planning Association) and the newly founded Allegheny Conference on Community Development. Along with the plans for a park, the Planning Association also wanted to develop the upper areas of the Point for newer commercial space. It contacted well-known Pittsburgh architect Ralph E. Griswold to help with finding a location for a new state office building at the Point. According to Griswold, it was he who suggested that the study for the office building also include a study for the potential

The Point in 1954, following the demolition and removal of the railroad properties and exposition buildings. The gingko trees stand guard around the Block House, with the caretaker's lodge remaining out front. *Courtesy of the Thomas & Katherine Detre Library and Archives, Sen. John Heinz History Center.*

of a state park at the Point. This suggestion was approved, and Griswold proceeded in his studies along with fellow architect Charles M. Stotz.[198]

Stotz and Griswold found themselves faced with the same problem as those before them: what to do with the bridges at the Point? They made two park designs—one design featured the bridges remaining in their original location, and the other featured the bridges pushed farther back toward the upper area of the Point. The second design allowed for much more park space, but it would also be more expensive to move the bridges away. These designs were presented to the governor of Pennsylvania,

Early brochure for the Fort Pitt Museum. The museum was built in conjunction with the construction of Point State Park, opening to the public in 1969. Still in operation today, the museum focuses on the early history of Pittsburgh and western Pennsylvania. *Courtesy of the Fort Pitt Society Collections.*

Edwin Martin, who ultimately chose the plan calling for the removal of the bridges at the Point. It was announced in October 1946 that the state would finance the building of Point State Park, committing $4 million toward the park's construction.[199]

It took two years for the Commonwealth of Pennsylvania to acquire the property for Point State Park. Despite this length of time, negotiations for the property seemed to go well. The Pennsylvania Railroad owned thirteen acres of land in the Point, and all thirteen acres were successfully acquired by the state through eminent domain by 1949. The rise of the automobile as the main mode of transportation in the United States had led to a decline in railroad transportation by the 1940s and 1950s. Although the Pennsylvania Railroad was still a viable corporation, it was not nearly as powerful as it had been fifty years before when it purchased the Point. This development, coupled with the rising interest in urban renewal, allowed for the relatively quiet takeover of the Point District by the Commonwealth of Pennsylvania.[200]

By May 1950, the demolition had begun, with wrecking balls tearing down the old railroad buildings and other dilapidated structures encompassing the historic Point. No dynamite or other blasting explosives were allowed to be used in the demolitions for fear that they would cause harm to the Block House—a significant turnaround from the days of the Pennsylvania Railroad's construction nearly fifty years before. There were plans to open a museum focusing on Fort Pitt and early Pittsburgh history; the museum would sit inside a reconstructed bastion of the fort. A "portal bridge" was to be constructed through the upper area of the Point; this bridge would serve as a connector for the Penn-Lincoln Highway, a new super highway that ultimately joined with the Pennsylvania Turnpike to the east of Pittsburgh. The Portal Bridge was completed in 1963, and it physically connected the Fort Pitt Bridge and the Fort Duquesne Bridge, two double-decker bridges that extended from the north (Fort Duquesne) and to the south and west (Fort Pitt). These bridges would replace the old Point and Manchester Bridges located at the tip of the Point. Once the old bridges were removed, a beautiful fountain would be constructed at the Point's apex—the crowning feature of the new Point State Park.[201]

A FEAR TAKES HOLD OF THE DAR

From the very beginning, the Fort Pitt Society of the Daughters of the American Revolution had a difficult time understanding exactly what was going to happen at the Point and, more importantly, what was going to happen to the Block House. The ladies were certainly at peace with the idea of a beautiful park replacing the ugliness that had surrounded their property for years. A park would only serve to better the conditions of the Block House, and it would increase visitation. When plans were made to conduct the archaeological excavations at the Point in 1941, the women supported the digs and allowed for test pits within the Block House yard.[202]

And yet, even as early as 1941—when the city was still in negotiations with the National Park Service—the Fort Pitt Society began to hear rumors that the Block House was in danger of being moved from its location as part of the plans of Point Park.[203] It had been more than thirty years since Edith Ammon's law was passed in state legislature, prohibiting the removal of the Block House by eminent domain. Hardly any Fort Pitt Society members who had participated in or witnessed the battles against the railroad were still alive by the 1940s and 1950s. (Edith Ammon had passed away in 1919.) Despite the lack of threats against the Block House's removal, the ladies still feared the day when someone—railroad, Schenley heirs or otherwise—would swoop down and take their Block House away. These fears, always lying beneath the skin, finally came to the surface with the planning of Point Park.

By December 1948, it had become clear that Point Park was to be constructed and operated by the Commonwealth of Pennsylvania. Rumors persisted among the ladies that it was the state's intention to claim ownership of the Block House through eminent domain. The Fort Pitt Society felt that the state could not legally take its property since the 1907 law protected the Block House from eminent domain; however, as the society's lawyer pointed out, the law only pertained to eminent domain as practiced by private corporations and businesses. The law did not apply to state government. The society's attorney insisted that the state had not announced any plans of taking the Block House property; if the women were to receive such notification from the Commonwealth, they were to let him know immediately.[204]

Nearly three years later, the ladies hired a different lawyer to represent them at meetings concerning the park and its construction. The fear of Block House removal, as well as a "takeover" by the Commonwealth of Pennsylvania, continued to haunt the Fort Pitt Society. At a society meeting held on October 10, 1951, a letter from the attorney general of Pennsylvania was read that assured the women that the park plans did not entail removing the Block House nor was there any intention by the state to gain title to the structure. This letter seemed to lessen the ladies' concerns, and they proceeded in negotiations and meetings with the Commonwealth and Point Park Commission. In January 1953, an agreement was signed between the society and the Commonwealth allowing for the demolition, excavation and removal of properties immediately surrounding the Block House. The agreement would help with any damage claims filed by the society as a result of the ongoing demolition around its property.[205]

Things seemed to be going relatively smoothly until the following autumn, when the Commonwealth made an offer to accept the Block House property as a gift from the society. The state would then operate the Block House as part of Point State Park. Not surprisingly, the society was entirely against the idea of the state owning and operating the Block House. The women of the Fort Pitt Society had fought long and hard to save the Block House and keep it open to visitors. They took seriously their mission to preserve, protect and promote the Block House as outlined in the deed they signed long ago in 1894. What would happen to the building if the state were to assume ownership? Would it be properly taken care of? Would it be moved elsewhere? The state was willing to have the society operate the building on behalf of the state, with the ladies retaining office space inside the soon-to-be constructed Fort Pitt Museum; however, this was also turned down by the society.[206]

Finally, in June 1954, another offer was made to the women. The Block House would remain under the ownership and operation of the Fort Pitt Society. In exchange for demolition of the old caretaker's lodge, the society would receive free office space inside the Fort Pitt Museum for the use of its caretaker. Not only would the state demolish the caretaker's lodge (without compensation to the society), but it would also receive ownership of the twenty- by ninety-foot strip of land on which the house stood. A cluster of gingko trees planted by the DAR in the early twentieth century would be removed from the Block House yard. The trees would be replaced with sugar maples, a tree native to eighteenth-century western Pennsylvania and in keeping with the landscaping scheme of the park.[207]

Although this newest offer retained DAR ownership of the Block House, the ladies were still not pleased. One of their major concerns was the demolition of the caretaker's lodge. Having the house on-site allowed for twenty-four-hour guarding of the Block House by the caretaker. If the caretaker could not be at the building at all times, there could be issues of

New skyscrapers and business centers were constructed alongside Point State Park as part of the overall renewal of the Point District. One such structure, the Westinghouse Building, rises up behind the Block House in this image from circa 1969. *Courtesy of the Thomas & Katherine Detre Library and Archives, Sen. John Heinz History Center.*

vandalism and fire. Whatever space the state intended to give the women inside the museum did not seem as adequate as their already-standing lodge. They argued that if they were to give up their lodge in exchange for the office space, they should be compensated for the loss of their property. The removal of the gingko trees also caused resentment among the society. The trees were planted at a time when little else would grow in the Point due to pollution. By the 1950s, they had become sentimental features to the ladies of the Fort Pitt Society, a memory of those who came before them. One aspect of the offer that appealed to the women was the exclusive right of the Fort Pitt Society to sell Block House souvenirs. This would prohibit the state from selling any Block House souvenirs from its new museum.[208] At the end of 1954, however, the ladies and the state had reached an impasse, and no further negotiations were conducted until 1960.

THE FIGHT AGAINST THE COMMONWEALTH

In early February 1959, there was a renewed interest on the part of the Fort Pitt Society to continue negotiations with the Commonwealth of Pennsylvania. The old concerns were still there, but a new board of directors was now in control. Since so many directors were recently elected, the board as a whole had little understanding or knowledge of the discussions held previously between the Point Park Commission and past Fort Pitt Society members.[209] This led to frustrations on both sides, especially with rumors continuing to fly about that the Commonwealth planned to take control of the Block House. This was actually not too far from the truth; by 1959, officials from both the Commonwealth and the Point Park Commission had grown weary of constant negotiating with the Fort Pitt Society. The state still held the upper hand over the society with the power of eminent domain, and it could invoke that power at any time. Despite this authority, the Commonwealth did not necessarily want to use eminent domain because it could backfire in public relations. How would it look for the government to seemingly "take away" the Fort Pitt Society's treasured property?[210]

It was not until November 2, 1960, that an official meeting was held between the Fort Pitt Society and the Point Park Commission. The commission, representing the interests of the Commonwealth of Pennsylvania and its Department of Forests and Waters, once again presented the plans for Point State Park, as well as the draft agreement for the Society to sign. Once again, the main issue for the society was the demolition of the caretaker's house. Although the commission reassured the ladies that there would be policemen monitoring the park both during and after its construction, the women were still afraid of what could happen to the Block House without a caretaker on-site at all times. This fear was relatively legitimate since at the time of the meeting, the park was still under construction with seemingly no end in sight. What if the caretaker's house was torn down but the park never completed? What if the next political elections brought in a new administration to Pennsylvania government—an administration that could very well cut the budget for the park? Not all of the ladies were against the demolition of the caretaker's house, with some agreeing that the time had come for it to be removed. The commission also stressed that previous Fort Pitt Society members had more or less allowed for its removal. The women strongly denied this claim, and in any case, those members were no longer part of the board of directors.[211]

The issue remained relatively quiet until two years later when the Point Park Commission submitted yet another proposal agreement to the Fort Pitt Society in January 1962. A succession of meetings and discussions was held throughout early 1962, with mostly all of them ending on the same issue of the caretaker's house. No agreement could be reached until the ladies allowed for its removal. It seemed as though the women became more and more steadfast in their determination not to have the building removed. When the commission insisted that the building was not in keeping with the theme of the park, the ladies offered to build a newer structure that would look like an eighteenth-century log cabin. The commission refused to entertain such an offer, especially since it was in the process of building the new Fort Pitt Museum, located directly across from the Block House. The society could maintain offices inside the museum, as well as use its boardrooms for meetings, thereby eliminating the need for any kind of separate building for its use. The women then asked if the proposed museum building could be used exclusively by the society to compensate for the loss of the caretaker's house; this offer was also refused since the main purpose of the new building was to be a public museum on the early history of Pittsburgh. With frustration growing by the day and the need for the park to be completed as soon as possible, the commission began to threaten condemnation of the Fort Pitt Society's property if the ladies did not come to an agreement. This threat only added fuel to the fire, and many of the women began to compare their fight with the state to their previous struggles with the Pennsylvania Railroad.[212]

The Fort Pitt Society Board of Directors once again changed hands in late spring of 1962. The newly elected board was different from those in the past in that it seemed less concerned with the actual removal of the caretaker's house and more concerned with how the Fort Pitt Society was to be compensated for such a removal. It was clear to the ladies of the society that if they did not give up their caretaker's house to the state, they risked losing everything, including their beloved Block House. If the state provided them with appropriate compensation for their loss of property, as well as allowed them office space in the new museum, an agreement would be considered. Maurice K. Goddard, the secretary of the Department of Forests and Waters in Pennsylvania, sent a letter to the Fort Pitt Society on June 22, 1962, with a final proposal for an agreement between the two entities. Similar to previous proposals, the Commonwealth of Pennsylvania would allow for the Fort Pitt Society to continue having full title to the Block House, as well as full control over its maintenance and operation. The society would turn over all of its property, including the caretaker's house, with the exception of the Block House and the fenced-in yard surrounding it. As compensation for the loss of property, the Commonwealth would allow for office space inside the museum along with access to boardrooms for meetings for the Fort Pitt

A view of Point State Park prior to the construction of the park's fountain. The Point Bridge (right) and Manchester Bridge (left) remained standing until 1965 as officials argued over who would pay for their removal. *Courtesy of the Thomas & Katherine Detre Library and Archives, Sen. John Heinz History Center.*

The long-awaited demolition of the caretaker's lodge in March 1966. In exchange for its demolition, the Fort Pitt Society was provided with office and storage space inside the new Fort Pitt Museum. *Courtesy of the Thomas & Katherine Detre Library and Archives, Sen. John Heinz History Center.*

Society. Finally, Goddard promised an increase in security around the Block House once the caretaker's house was demolished.[213]

Although the Fort Pitt Society generally approved of Goddard's proposal, there were still concerns over compensation for the caretaker's house, as well as concern for the gingko trees surrounding the Block House. At a meeting held in September 1962, the issue of the gingko trees came to a head. The ladies were strongly opposed to their removal since they had been planted by early society members. The trees had become a symbol of their legacy with the Block House, a representation of their determination to save a little piece of Pittsburgh's history and improve its landscape. The architects of the park, especially Ralph Griswold, persisted that the trees needed to be removed since they would not have been at the Point in the eighteenth century. Griswold even went so far as to say that no agreement would be made with the society if they did not allow for the removal of the gingkoes. In response to this demand, the ladies pointed out that not everything in the park would be in keeping with the eighteenth century anyway, especially the grand fountain planned for the Point's apex. According to minutes from the meeting, the women stated that "the proposed [park] fountain at the Point would not be in keeping with this area in 1764, and this statement brought forth an outburst from Mr. Griswold that was ill-advised and undeserved."[214] Apparently, tensions had reached an all-time high between the Park Commission and the Fort Pitt Society.

The meeting ended with the women very much afraid that the state would take their property simply because of the gingko trees. The threats made by Griswold over the trees had left them shaken to the point that they actually decided to have one of the directors meet with Maurice Goddard personally over the matter. This one-on-one encounter with Secretary Goddard proved to be successful. Goddard's main concern at this time was that the park and museum be completed as soon as possible. The sooner the Fort Pitt Society signed an agreement, the sooner the caretaker's house could be demolished and work on the park could continue. He certainly was not going to let a few gingko trees stand in the way of this progress. He willingly allowed for the trees to remain standing so long as a final agreement could be reached on the caretaker's house.[215]

An Agreement Is Reached

Now that the gingko trees' futures were secured, an agreement could finally be made between the Commonwealth and the Fort Pitt Society. It was a long time in coming, but on June 25, 1963, an option for the twenty-by-ninety feet of property owned by the society (which included the caretaker's house) was signed between the ladies and the Department of Forests and Waters. The state agreed to a purchase price for the land of $50,000, which would go to the Fort Pitt Society. The option agreement also stipulated that the Fort Pitt Society would have free office space in the Fort Pitt Museum for its caretaker, as well as access to the museum's conference rooms for meetings. It was agreed that the society's caretaker would continue to occupy the house until the office space was completed inside the museum. Once the office was finished, the caretaker's house would be demolished. The society would

The Fort Pitt Museum was formally dedicated and opened to the public in 1969. Here is an image taken around that time with the Block House and its ground in front of the new museum. The museum is now operated by the Senator John Heinz History Center. *Courtesy of the Thomas & Katherine Detre Library and Archives, Sen. John Heinz History Center.*

have the perpetual right to sell souvenirs related to the Block House, with those sales being conducted inside the Block House or in such other place(s) that the society and the Commonwealth would agree to in the future. The Commonwealth agreed to provide constant security for the Block House free of charge; the society agreed to bear the cost of redeveloping its remaining ninety- by one-hundred-foot property in accordance with the park construction. The gingko trees would remain in place. The deed for the caretaker's house and property was formally signed in August 1963.

By 1969, progress had been accomplished in Point State Park. The caretaker's house was demolished, and the Fort Pitt Museum was completed and opened to the public. The beautiful fountain at the tip of the Point was finished in 1974, whereupon the park was formally dedicated.[216] Since the early nineteenth century, the people of Pittsburgh dreamed of a park at the Point in which they could enjoy their city and commemorate their earliest history. More than one hundred years in the making, Point State Park would now serve as a place for all to come and learn about Fort Duquesne and Fort Pitt, as well as for the citizens of Pittsburgh to stand back and view the beautiful city they called home. At the heart of this park would be the Fort Pitt Block House, a monument to the test of time.

THE BLOCK HOUSE TODAY

Over the past four decades, the Point has become one of the leading destinations for citizens and tourists in Pittsburgh. People come to see the fountain, the Fort Pitt Museum and the tiny yet sturdy Fort Pitt Block House. Surrounded by the tranquility of the park, the historic Block House is part of the Forks of the Ohio National Historic Landmark, as well as the Pittsburgh Renaissance Historic District on the National Register of Historic Places. It was designated as a Historical Landmark by the Pittsburgh History and Landmarks Foundation in 2008. Numerous preservation and restoration projects have been conducted on the building over the years, most recently in 2007 and 2013. In 2007, the building received a new roof, a French drain system around its perimeter and new landscaping. Restoration and preservation of the Block House's original gun loop timbers were the main focuses of the 2013 project, with the novel use of X-ray imaging to help locate severely rotted areas inside the timbers. Minor repairs to the building's masonry were also conducted as part of the project.[217] All

Postcard image of Point State Park shortly after its completion. *Courtesy of the Fort Pitt Society Collections.*

of these projects continue to be administered by the Fort Pitt Society of the Daughters of the American Revolution of Allegheny County, Pennsylvania (the Pittsburgh Chapter of the NSDAR) through private funding and the support of the community.

The Block House has been flooded numerous times, including the infamous St. Patrick's Day Flood of 1936. Considered the worst flood in Pittsburgh's history with a 46.4-foot crest above normal pool, the 1936 Flood actually reached above the roof of the Block House! Most recently, in 2004, the Block House had water in its lower floor, nearly reaching the first set of gun loop timbers. Flooding remains a constant threat to both the Block House and the Point; however, flood controls built throughout western Pennsylvania in the 1950s and 1960s have greatly altered the height and damage of the floods.[218]

Despite flooding, restoration and being used as someone's house for more than one hundred years, the Block House remains largely intact, with approximately 80 percent of its bricks, stone and wood still dating to 1764. It has never been moved from its location—a 250-year-old witness to Pittsburgh's incredible history. Tens of thousands of visitors come to see the Block House every year from all over the United States and around the

Above: The St. Patrick's Day Flood of 1936 is still the considered the worst flood in Pittsburgh's history, cresting 46.4 feet above normal pool levels. At the height of the flood, the Block House was almost completely submerged under water. This postcard image shows the water receded to the top of the door of the Block House. *Courtesy of the Fort Pitt Society Collections.*

Left: The Fort Pitt Block House as it appears today. *Photo by Kelly Linn, courtesy of the Fort Pitt Society Collections.*

world. On July 4, 2013, the Block House received 3,123 visitors, one of the busiest days the building has ever experienced. A third-grade student visiting the Block House in the spring of 2013 had this to say about her trip:

> *My favorite place where I went was the Fort Pitt Block House because it is so amazing. Just think how many stories came from the Block House! I think it is very fascinating. It was the best.*[219]

This happy statement from such a young voice proves that the Block House continues to thrive with new generations eager to learn the story it has to tell. For decades, people have remarked on its significance and fought for its survival. It is amazing to think of such a tiny building captivating so many people. Forts were built and torn down within thirty years. Housing and factories were built and torn down within a century. Powerful corporations constructed large rail yards and industrial warehouses—only to have them torn down within fifty years. But the Fort Pitt Block House remains standing, and it will remain for generations to come.

Notes

Prologue

1. The Six Nations consisted of the Seneca, Onondaga, Cayuga, Mohawk, Oneida and Tuscarora tribes. Anderson, *Crucible of War*, 12, 748.
2. James, "Decision at the Forks," *Drums in the Forest*, 21.
3. Anderson, *Crucible of War*, 27.
4. James, "Decision at the Forks," 24–26.
5. Stotz, *Outposts of the War for Empire*, 11–15.
6. Ibid., 11–15.
7. Dixon, *Never Come to Peace Again*, 34–35.
8. Ibid., 47, 48; Stevens, "Unknown Author: Extract of a Letter from Pittsburgh (Lately Fort Duquesne), November 26, 1758; First Published in *Pennsylvania Gazette*, December 14, 1758," *Papers of Henry Bouquet*, vol. 2, 612–13.
9. Forbes, originally from Scotland, pronounced Pittsburgh as "Pittsboro," similar to the spelling and pronunciation of Edinburgh, Scotland.
10. Stotz, "Defense in the Wilderness," *Drums in the Forest*, 160, 161–64.
11. Waddell, "Bouquet to J. Amherst, January 12, 1762," *Papers of Henry Bouquet*, vol. 6, 36–37.
12. Ibid., 36–37; Waddell, "S. Ecuyer to Bouquet, March 11, 1763," *Papers of Henry Bouquet*, vol. 6, 167–68; Stotz, *Outposts of the War for Empire*, 136.
13. Anderson, *Crucible of War*, 278–79.
14. Crytzer, *Fort Pitt*, 43.

15. Ibid., 87.
16. Ibid., 88.
17. Waddell, "S. Ecuyer to Bouquet, May 30, 1763," *Papers of Henry Bouquet*, vol. 6, 195–96.
18. Dixon, *Never Come to Peace Again*, 136–37, 139.
19. Ibid., 43–45.
20. Crytzer, *Fort Pitt*, 74, 77.
21. Dixon, *Never Come to Peace Again*, 158, 168.
22. Ibid., 182–84.
23. Ibid., 185, 190–91, 195.

Chapter 1

24. Waddell, "Bouquet to Gage, December 27, 1763," *Papers of Henry Bouquet*, vol. 6, 486.
25. Dunnigan, *Forts Within a Fort*, 5, 7.
26. Ibid., 5–6.
27. Ibid., 8.
28. Ibid.
29. Stotz, *Outposts of the War for Empire*, 137.
30. Waddell, "W. Grant to Bouquet, May 15, 1764," *Papers of Henry Bouquet*, vol. 6, 541.
31. Craig, *History of Pittsburgh*, 72, 271.
32. What is being referred to as the "back wall" is today considered the front of the Block House since it is the location of its modern-day entrance door.
33. Clark, *Fort Pitt Block House Conditions Survey*, 5–6.
34. Wagner, "Men from Early Middle Ages."
35. Clark, *Fort Pitt Block House Conditions Survey*, 9.
36. Ibid., 6.
37. Michael Baker Inc., *Archaeological Excavations in the Fort Pitt Block House*, 30.
38. McDonald, "Castle Architecture."
39. Clark, *Fort Pitt Block House Conditions Survey*, 12.
40. The artwork referred to is an 1832 drawing by Russell Smith. Smith later produced an oil painting based on his original sketch. Because of its significance to understanding the early history of the Block House, it will be discussed extensively later in this book.
41. Anderson, *Crucible of War*, 565–66.

42. National Park Service, "1768 Boundary Line Treaty of Fort Stanwix."
43. Crytzer, *Fort Pitt*, 128.
44. McClure, *Ohio Country Missionary*, 101.
45. *Minutes of the Provincial Council of Pennsylvania*, 68–69, 71, 74–75.
46. Hazard, *Pennsylvania Archives*, vol. 10, series 1, 463–64.
47. Nelson, *Man of Distinction Among Them*, 1, 62–63.
48. Ibid., 66.
49. Michael Baker Inc., *Archaeological Excavations in the Fort Pitt Block House*, 82, 99.
50. Crytzer, *Fort Pitt*, 139–40.
51. Dahlinger, *Fort Pitt*, 33–35.
52. Ibid., 36–37, 39.
53. Nelson, *Man of Distinction Among Them*, 101–3.
54. Hazard, *Pennsylvania Archives*, vol. 12, series 1, 133.

CHAPTER 2

55. Dahlinger, *Fort Pitt*, 57.
56. Ibid., 57–59; Allegheny County Deed Book, vol. 4, 299, 304.
57. Allegheny County Deed Book, vol. 4, 299, 302, 304; Westmoreland County Deed Book, vol. A, 528.
58. Williams, *American Pioneer*, vol. 1, 238–39.
59. Pawlikowski, "From the Bottom Up," 207–8.
60. Ibid., 21, 26, 50, 77, 105–9, 116–17.
61. This was the same John Neville who had commanded Fort Pitt following Dunmore's War. He owned a large plantation named Bower Hill, as well as many other properties throughout the Pittsburgh area. He later became known for his role in the Whiskey Rebellion.
62. Dahlinger, *Fort Pitt*, 57.
63. Pawlikowski, "From the Bottom Up," 170, 180, 183.
64. Ibid., 184, 196.
65. Ibid., 191.
66. Egle, "Letter-Book of Major Isaac Craig, III," 123; Egle, "Major Isaac Craig," 298.
67. Pawlikowski, "From the Bottom Up," 192–93; Allegheny County Deed Book, vol. 4, 306.
68. Shiras, *Justice George Shiras, Jr. of Pittsburgh*, 2.

69. These writers include Charles Dahlinger, Stanley Baron (*Brewing in America*) and John W. Jordan. They all cite the 1795 article, or they cite an author who in turn used the article.
70. Allegheny County Deed Book, vol. 9, 21; Allegheny County Deed Book, vol. 9, 23; Shiras, *Justice George Shiras, Jr. of Pittsburgh*, 4.
71. Jordan, *Colonial and Revolutionary Families of Pennsylvania*, vol. 3, 1,574–76.
72. Shiras, *Justice George Shiras, Jr. of Pittsburgh*, 3–4.
73. Allegheny County Deed Book, vol. 13, 220; Shiras, *Justice George Shiras, Jr. of Pittsburgh*, 6–8.
74. Boucher, *Century and a Half of Pittsburgh and Her People*, vol. 2, 404–5.
75. Shiras, *Justice George Shiras, Jr. of Pittsburgh*, 8–9.
76. Baron, *Brewing in America*, 131–34.
77. Dorr, *Memoir of John F. Watson*, 18; Watson, *Annals of Philadelphia and Pennsylvania*, vol. 2, 131.
78. Michael Baker Inc., *Archaeological Excavations in the Fort Pitt Block House*, 64–66.
79. Allegheny County Deed Book, vol. 13, 221.
80. Boucher, *Century and a Half of Pittsburgh and Her People*, vol. 2, 406.
81. A map of Pittsburgh in 1835 shows the new location of the Shiras Brewery at Pitt Street, a few blocks up from the Point District (Darlington Digital Library Maps, University of Pittsburgh). An 1837 Pittsburgh City Directory also lists the brewery as moving to "Pitt near Penn Street." *Harris' Pittsburgh Business Directory for the Year 1837* (Pittsburgh, PA: Isaac Harris, 1837). Republished by University of Pittsburgh Digital Research Library, 1999, http://digital.library.pitt.edu/cgi-bin/t/text/text-idx?idno=00afv6656m;view=toc;c=pitttextdir, 149.
82. Watson, *Annals of Philadelphia and Pennsylvania*, vol. 2, 131.
83. Lyford, *Western Address Directory*, 45–46.
84. Fahnestock, "Note to Map," *Fahnestock's Pittsburgh Directory for 1850* (Pittsburgh, PA: George Parkin & Company, 1850). Republished by University of Pittsburgh Digital Research Library, 2008, http://digital.library.pitt.edu/cgi-bin/t/text/text-idx?idno=31735055723096;view=toc;c=pitttextdir, iv.
85. Ferguson, *America by River and Rail*, 246–47.
86. This is based largely on an original 1843 drawing by Sherman Day from his *Historical Collections of the State of Pennsylvania*.
87. Lambing, *History of the Catholic Church*, 138.
88. Dahlinger, *Fort Pitt*, 77; *Pittsburgh Gazette Times*, December 24, 1911; *Pittsburg and Allegheny Directory, 1899* (Pittsburgh, PA: R.L. Polk & Company,

1899). Republished by University of Pittsburgh Digital Research Library, 2008, http://digital.library.pitt.edu/cgi-bin/t/text/text-idx?idno=31735055723310;view=toc;c=pitttextdir, 950.

89. *Directory of Pittsburgh and Allegheny Cities, 1863/1864* (Pittsburgh, PA: G.H. Thurston, 1863). Republished by University of Pittsburgh Digital Research Library, 2008, http://digital.library.pitt.edu/cgi-bin/t/text/text-idx?idno=31735055723104;view=toc;c=pitttextdir, 246.

90. *Pittsburgh Telegraph*, "Old Block House Occupant Dies," June 1, 1914, under "The Point," Carnegie Library of Pittsburgh website; *Pittsburgh Press*, "Body of Pioneer Woman Will Be Buried Here," June 2, 1914.

91. *Pittsburgh Post-Gazette*, "Old Resident Dies in Northside Home," January 15, 1935; United States Census 1860, University of Pittsburgh Digital Library, http://digital.library.pitt.edu/cgi-bin/census/census_driver.pl?searchtype=household&key_1=1788&key_2=1&database=Pittsburgh_1860; *Directory of Pittsburgh and Its Vicinity for the Year 1859–1860* (Pittsburgh, PA: George H. Thurston, 1859). Republished by University of Pittsburgh Digital Research Library, 2008, http://digital.library.pitt.edu/cgi-bin/t/text/text-idx?idno=31735055723062;view=toc;c=pitttextdir, 47.

92. Muller, "City of Pittsburgh," 51.

93. 1880 United States Census, available at Ancestry.com.

94. Bliss, for the Point Park Commission "Part One of the Report of the Point Park Commission," 92.

95. *Pittsburgh Post*, "Farewell to the Old Fort," April 23, 1894.

96. This may have been a minor error on Sibby's part since there is a letter dated April 4, 1894, from the agent of the Schenley estate stating that an "S. Powers," living in the downstairs floor of the Block House, paid four dollars monthly rent, not five dollars, to the building's lease-owner, T. Maddon (who, in turn, leased it from the Schenley estate).

97. Bliss, for the Point Park Commission "Part One of the Report of the Point Park Commission," 92.

98. Business Men's Protective Association, *A Confidential Business Report of Pittsburgh and Allegheny, 1878* (Pittsburgh, PA: W.P. Bennett, 1878). Republished by University of Pittsburgh Digital Research Library, 2008, http://digital.library.pitt.edu/cgi-bin/t/text/text-idx?idno=31735055723062;view=toc;c=pitttextdir, 150.

99. 1880 United States Census, available at Ancestry.com.

100. All directory information was collected from the Historic Pittsburgh website, hosted by the University of Pittsburgh Digital Research Library. This site features digitized copies of almost every city directory for

Pittsburgh from the mid-nineteenth century into the early twentieth century. http://digital.library.pitt.edu/cgi-bin/t/text/text-idx?c=pitttext dir;page=browse;key=date.

101. *Pittsburgh Press*, "Woman Who Lived in Old Blockhouse Never Returns," July 31, 1933, under "The Point," Carnegie Library of Pittsburgh website.

102. *Pittsburgh Post-Gazette*, "Played in the Blockhouse," May 11, 1935.

103. Water, *Don't Call Me Boss*, 9, 41.

104. Michael Baker Inc., *Archaeological Excavations in the Fort Pitt Block House*, 33.

105. This tablet still exists today (although in a different location), and it has sparked many questions over the years as to whether it is original to the structure. While it cannot be denied that it is a very old stone based on its condition and the script engraved on its surface, it is also important to remember how the Block House was originally used. Would the soldiers have taken the time to create such a stone for a rather insignificant structure? Is it more likely that someone from the late eighteenth century decided to make the tablet as a marker to the past?

106. Bliss, for the Point Park Commission "Part One of the Report of the Point Park Commission," 92.

107. Ibid.

108. *Minutes from the DAR of Allegheny County, 1893–1894*, minutes from June 19, 1894, Fort Pitt Society Collections.

109. *Harper's Weekly*, "Centennial Celebration at Pittsburgh, Pennsylvania," 773–74; *Pittsburgh Leader Almanac for 1872*, frontispiece.

CHAPTER 3

110. Salisbury, "Pittsburgh's Great Romance," 343–54; Marie McSwigan, "Stanton Heights Golf Links Is Shrine of City's History," *Pittsburgh Press*, November 2, 1929.

111. Storey, *To the Golden Land*, 96.

112. This city hall was in use until 1917, when the current City-County Building was constructed; the former city hall was demolished in 1952.

113. Allegheny County Board of Commissioners, *City Hall, Pittsburgh Cornerstone Laid*, 28, 30.

114. George Swetnam, "The Man Who Saved the Blockhouse," *Pittsburgh Press*, September 20, 1959.

115. West, *Domesticating History*, 43.

116. Meeting minutes mention that the "Block House committee's" report was still being finalized. They were most likely waiting for Schenley's response, which did not arrive until nearly two months later. *Minutes 1891–1897 Pittsburgh Chapter D.A.R.*, minutes from March 25, 1892, 9, Fort Pitt Society Collections.
117. Amelia Neville Shields Oliver to Mary Elizabeth Schenley, undated, Fort Pitt Society Collections.
118. Ibid.
119. Mary Elizabeth Schenley to Amelia Neville Shields Oliver, May 23, 1892, Fort Pitt Society Collections; *Minutes 1891–1897 Pittsburgh Chapter D.A.R.*, minutes from June 10, 1892, 14–15.
120. Mary Elizabeth Schenley to Amelia Neville Shields Oliver, August 23, 1892, Fort Pitt Society Collections; *Minutes 1891–1897 Pittsburgh Chapter D.A.R.*, minutes from September 23, 1892, 18.
121. *Minutes 1891–1897 Pittsburgh Chapter D.A.R.*, minutes from September 23, 1892, 16–19, Pittsburgh Chapter NSDAR Collections.
122. Allegheny County Court Book, vol. 18, 259–64; Allegheny County Court Book, vol. 52, 56–57.
123. *Minutes from the DAR of Allegheny County, 1893–1894*, minutes from November 9, 1893, and December 9, 1893, Fort Pitt Society Collections.
124. Herron & Sons to Matilda Denny, December 8, 1893, Fort Pitt Society Collections.
125. Deed to Block House Property, Mary E. Schenley to Daughters of the American Revolution of Allegheny County, Pennsylvania, recorded April 28, 1894, Fort Pitt Society Collections.
126. Ibid.
127. Ibid.
128. Ibid.
129. William A. Herron to Captain W.F. Aull, April 4, 1894, Fort Pitt Society Collections.
130. Ibid.
131. *Pittsburgh Post*, "Home of History: The Old Blockhouse Turned Over to the Daughters of the Revolution," April 15, 1894.
132. *Pittsburgh Post*, "Tenants Ready to Leave: Sorrowful Exodus from the Old Blockhouse," April 28, 1894.
133. *Pittsburgh Post*, "Farewell to the Old Fort: People of the Point Weep Over Coming Changes," April 23, 1894.
134. *Pittsburgh Post*, "Tenants Ready to Leave," April 28, 1894.
135. *Pittsburgh Post*, "Farewell to the Old Fort," April 23, 1894.

136. *Minutes from the DAR of Allegheny County, 1893–1894*, minutes from May 14, 1894; *Pittsburgh Press*, "Obituary, Matthew Golden," September 27, 1901.
137. *Minutes from the DAR of Allegheny County, 1893–1894*, minutes from June 5, 1894.
138. *Pittsburgh Post*, "The Third Anniversary: Daughters of the American Revolution Celebrate It," June 12, 1894.
139. *Minutes from the DAR of Allegheny County, 1893–1894*, minutes from June 11, 1894.
140. Clark, *Fort Pitt Block House Conditions Survey*, 12.
141. Ibid., 9–10, 12–13.
142. Ibid., 14, 16.
143. *Minutes from the DAR of Allegheny County, 1893–1894*; *Minutes from the DAR of Allegheny County, 1894–1902*, minutes from December 8, 1894, and January 26, 1895, Fort Pitt Society Collections.
144. The sundial is an artifact shrouded in mystery. Other than the obvious reason of commemoration, it is not known why such a sundial was created or for whom it was created. The sundial was ultimately loaned to the new Carnegie Museum in Pittsburgh, where it remained until 1916. It was brought back to the Block House property, where it was put on display outside, open to the elements. Eventually, a glass (and later Plexiglas) case covered the stone, but pollution and weathering had taken their toll. In 2006, the sundial was moved into a display case located inside the Block House. It was professionally conserved in 2010, whereupon it was suggested to remove the sundial from the Block House and place it into storage in the Fort Pitt Society's collection space inside the nearby Fort Pitt Museum. Recently, in 2012, the sundial was put on display inside the Fort Pitt Museum as part of a loan from the Fort Pitt Society. The sundial will remain as a semipermanent exhibit in the museum, where it can be viewed properly by visitors. All information on the sundial taken from *Fort Pitt Sundial Condition Report*, updated July 2012, and *Fort Pitt Sundial Conservation Report*, Teresa S. Duff, October 18, 2010, Fort Pitt Society Collections.
145. *Minutes from the DAR of Allegheny County, 1894–1902*, minutes from October 11, 1895, and June 8, 1896.
146. *Minutes from the DAR of Allegheny County, 1894–1902*, minutes from May 15, 1900, and June 9, 1900.
147. The current Sixth Street Bridge is commonly called the Roberto Clemente Bridge as it leads to PNC Park, the home of the Pittsburgh Pirates baseball team. The Clemente Bridge is the fourth bridge in that span. *Minutes from the DAR of Allegheny County, 1894–1902*, minutes from May 5, 1898.

148. Daughters of the American Revolution of Allegheny County, Pennsylvania. *Fort Duquesne and Fort Pitt*, 37–38.
149. *Minutes from the DAR of Allegheny County, 1894–1902*, minutes from December 6, 1901, and December 13, 1901.
150. Ibid.
151. Linn, "Patriotism Wins."
152. *Minutes from the DAR of Allegheny County, 1894–1902*, minutes from December 13, 1901.
153. Franklin F. Nicola to J. Harvey White, December 13, 1901, Fort Pitt Society Collections.
154. *Pittsburgh Chapter NSDAR/Fort Pitt Society Scrapbook, 1901–1902*, 5, Fort Pitt Society Collections.
155. For a period of time in Pittsburgh's history, the mayor was called the "recorder." Joseph O. Brown therefore would have been the equivalent of the mayor of Pittsburgh at the time he met with the Fort Pitt Society.
156. *Minutes from the DAR of Allegheny County, 1894–1902*, minutes from December 19, 1901; *Scrapbook, 1901–1902*, 2.
157. Fleming, *History of Pittsburgh and Environs*, vol. 4, 96–97.
158. Jordan, *Colonial and Revolutionary Families of Pennsylvania*, vol. 3, 1,544–46.
159. Reed, *Century Cyclopedia of History & Biography*, vol. 2, 99–101; Fleming, *History of Pittsburgh and Environs*, vol. 4, 189–90.
160. Davis, *Reminiscences of General William Larimer*, 20, 21, 99; Fleming, *History of Pittsburgh and Environs*, vol. 4, 313.
161. The estate was named after Guyasuta, a Mingo/Seneca leader who traveled with George Washington in 1753 and later went up against the British on the Pennsylvania frontier during Pontiac's War. Following the American Revolution, James O'Hara invited the aging Guyasuta to live the rest of his days on the O'Hara estate along the Allegheny River. It was here where Guyasuta died in 1803; he was also buried on the property. His grave was removed years later in 1918 when the Pennsylvania Railroad purchased the estate from the Darlington family. His remains were supposedly given to the Carnegie Museum of Natural History in Pittsburgh. There are also claims that he was reburied along French Creek above the Allegheny River. Galloway, "Guyasuta," 20–21, 27.
162. Herbert, *Personal Memories of the Darlington Family*, 17–24.
163. Darlington Digital Library, University of Pittsburgh, http://digital.library.pitt.edu/d/darlington/index.html.
164. Ammon, *Pittsburgh Chapter D.A.R.*, Fort Pitt Society Collections.

165. *Scrapbook, 1901–1902*, 32. Taken from a newspaper clipping from the *Pittsburgh Leader*, January 16, 1902.
166. *Scrapbook, 1901–1902*, 32–33.
167. Ibid., 34.
168. Ibid., 29, 40.
169. *Minutes from the DAR of Allegheny County, 1894–1902*, minutes from February 6 and February 13, 1902.
170. "Report to the Members of the Pittsburgh Chapter, Daughters of the American Revolution, Given by the Board of Directors of the Daughters of the American Revolution of Allegheny County, PA, and the Advisory Committee of the Pittsburgh Chapter NSDAR," February 1, 1905, Fort Pitt Society Collections.
171. *Minutes from the DAR of Allegheny County, 1894–1902*, minutes from February 14, 1902, and March 29, 1902.
172. The exposition buildings consisted of three structures built for the Pittsburgh Exposition Society in 1889. They were used for various expositions, fairs, exhibitions and other events throughout the nineteenth and twentieth centuries. They stood along the Allegheny River at the Point. By the 1950s, the exposition buildings were being used as automobile pounds.
173. *Scrapbook, 1901–1902*, 84, 93, 96, 100.
174. *Daughters of the American Revolution of Allegheny County, Pennsylvania v. Mary E. Schenley, Frank F. Nicola, John W. Herron, and the City of Pittsburgh*, Court of Common Pleas No. 2 of Allegheny County, No. 513, April Term, 1902, Fort Pitt Society Collections.
175. *Daughters of the American Revolution of Allegheny County, Pennsylvania v. Mary E. Schenley, Frank F. Nicola, John W. Herron, and the City of Pittsburgh*, appealed to the Supreme Court of Pennsylvania, November 1902, Fort Pitt Society Collections.
176. *Scrapbook, 1901–1902*, 53, 82.
177. Ibid., 117; Boucher, *Century and a Half of Pittsburgh and Her People*, vol. 2, 451.
178. *Scrapbook, 1901–1902*, 116; Boucher, *Century and a Half of Pittsburgh and Her People*, vol. 2, 451.
179. *Scrapbook, 1903–1906*, 9.
180. Ibid., 11, 13; *Minutes from the DAR of Allegheny County, 1902–1905*, minutes from April 3, 1903.
181. *Scrapbook, 1903–1906*, 23.
182. Ibid., 23, 25.
183. Ibid., 22–23, 35, 45; *Minutes from the DAR of Allegheny County, 1902–1905*, minutes from April 25, 1903.

184. *Minutes from the DAR of Allegheny County, 1902–1905*, minutes from April 25, 1903.
185. "Report to the Members of the Pittsburgh Chapter…," February 1, 1905; "Statement of the President, Annual Meeting of the Daughters of the American Revolution of Allegheny County, Pennsylvania," report given by Edith Ammon, June 2, 1911, Fort Pitt Society Collections.
186. "Report to the Members of the Pittsburgh Chapter…," February 1, 1905.
187. *Minutes from the DAR of Allegheny County, 1902–1905*, minutes from October 4, 1904; November 4, 1904; December 2, 1904; and December 15, 1904.
188. *Minutes from the DAR of Allegheny County, 1902–1905*, minutes from September 26, 1905, and October 6, 1905.
189. *Minutes from the DAR of Allegheny County, 1902–1905*, minutes from May 8, 1905.
190. "Edith Ammon's Law," Fort Pitt Society Collections.
191. "Annual Report 1907," *Minutes of from the DAR of Allegheny County, 1906–1911*, Fort Pitt Society Collections.
192. "Statement of the President," June 2, 1911.
193. "Statement of the Regent, Annual Meeting of the Pittsburgh Chapter NSDAR," report given by Edith Ammon, June 6, 1902, Fort Pitt Society Collections.

CHAPTER 4

194. Alberts, *Shaping of the Point*, 39–42.
195. Ibid., 43.
196. Ibid., 44–46.
197. Alberts, *Shaping of the Point*, 56; Bliss, for the Point Park Commission "Part One of the Report of the Point Park Commission."
198. Alberts, *Shaping of the Point*, 68–69.
199. Ibid., 71, 77–79.
200. Ibid., 99.
201. Ibid., 108, 110, 164.
202. Willard H. Buente, Point Park Commission and Chief Engineer for City Planning Commission, to Amelia Crittenden, president of the Fort Pitt Society, April 1, 1942, Fort Pitt Society Collections; Agreement between the Fort Pitt Society of the Daughters of the American Revolution and

the City of Pittsburgh for Archaeological Excavations, April 13, 1942, Fort Pitt Society Collections.

203. Hill Burgwin, attorney for Fort Pitt Society, to Amelia Crittenden, president of the Fort Pitt Society, January 6, 1941, Fort Pitt Society Collections; Hill Burgwin, attorney for Fort Pitt Society, to Edwin B. Graham, secretary of Pittsburgh Sons of the American Revolution, January 6, 1941, Fort Pitt Society Collections.

204. Theodore L. Hazlett Jr. to Winifred Jones Lucci, officer of the Fort Pitt Society, December 10, 1948, Fort Pitt Society Collections.

205. *Minutes of the Fort Pitt Society DAR of Allegheny County, PA, January 24, 1951, to April 1, 1959*, January 28, 1953, Fort Pitt Society Collections.

206. Alberts, *Shaping of the Point*, 168.

207. Copy of third draft of agreement between the Fort Pitt Society of the Daughters of the American Revolution and the Department of Forests and Waters of the Commonwealth of Pennsylvania, composed by Theodore L. Hazlett Jr., June 21, 1954, Fort Pitt Society Collections.

208. Ibid.

209. *Meeting of the Board of the Fort Pitt Society of the Daughters of the American Revolution of Allegheny County, Pennsylvania, Wednesday Morning, February 11, 1959*, Fort Pitt Society Collections.

210. Alberts, *Shaping of the Point*, 172.

211. *Minutes of the Fort Pitt Society DAR of Allegheny County, PA, May 5, 1959, to April 17, 1965*, November 2, 1960.

212. *Minutes of the Fort Pitt Society DAR of Allegheny County, PA, May 5, 1959, to April 17, 1965*, January 5, 1962–April 2, 1962.

213. Maurice K. Goddard to Elinor McConnell, president of the Fort Pitt Society, June 22, 1962, Fort Pitt Society Collections.

214. *Minutes of the Fort Pitt Society DAR of Allegheny County, PA, May 5, 1959, to April 17, 1965*, September 11, 1962.

215. *Minutes of the Fort Pitt Society DAR of Allegheny County, PA, May 5, 1959, to April 17, 1965*, September 26, 1962, and January 23, 1963.

216. Alberts, *Shaping of the Point*, 1–9.

217. Fort Pitt Block House, "Preservation & Restoration."

218. "Flood Marks for the Fort Pitt Block House," Fort Pitt Society Collections.

219. *Pittsburgh Places and Character-Building Words*, 23.

Bibliography

Primary Sources

Manuscript Materials

Fort Pitt Society Collections. Including letters of correspondence, scrapbooks, meeting minutes, reports and other archival materials. Office of the Fort Pitt Society of the Daughters of the American Revolution of Allegheny County, Pennsylvania, Pittsburgh, Pennsylvania.

Printed Materials

Allegheny County Board of Commissioners. *The City Hall, Pittsburgh Cornerstone Laid, May 5, 1869, Dedicated, May 23, 1872*. Pittsburgh, PA: Stevenson & Foster, 1874. Republished by University of Pittsburgh Digital Research Library, 1999. http://digital.library.pitt.edu/cgi-bin/t/text/text-idx?idno=00awn7796m;view=toc;c=pitttext.

Allegheny County Deed Books, vols. 4, 9 and 13. Allegheny County Department of Real Estate.

Ammon, Edith Darlington. *The Pittsburgh Chapter D.A.R.: A Review of Ten Years, 1899–1909.* Pittsburgh, PA: privately printed, 1909.

Bliss, Wesley L., for the Point Park Commission. "Part One of the Report of the Point Park Commission of Pittsburgh, Pennsylvania." Pittsburgh, PA: privately printed, 1944.

Clark, Mark D. *The Fort Pitt Block House Conditions Survey & Preliminary Restoration Plan*. Roanoke, VA: Southwest Restoration. Condition survey report given to the Fort Pitt Society of the Daughters of the American Revolution of Allegheny County, Pennsylvania, March 2011.

Daughters of the American Revolution of Allegheny County, Pennsylvania. *Fort Duquesne and Fort Pitt*. Pittsburgh, PA: privately printed, 1899.

Dorr, Benjamin. *A Memoir of John F. Watson*. Philadelphia, PA: Collins, 1861. Google e-book.

Egle, William H., ed. "Letter-Book of Major Isaac Craig, III: Craig to General Knox, May 13, 1792." *Historical Register* 2, no. 4 (December 1884). Google e-book.

———. "Major Isaac Craig: Extracts from His Letter-Books While Quartermaster at Fort Pitt, 1791–1804: Craig to General Knox, October 6, 1791." *Historical Register* 1, no. 4 (December 1883). Google e-book.

Ferguson, William. *America by River and Rail*. London: James Nisbet & Company, 1856. Google e-book.

Harper's Weekly. "The Centennial Celebration at Pittsburgh, Pennsylvania" (December 4, 1858): 773–74.

Hazard, Samuel, ed. *Pennsylvania Archives: Selected and Arranged from Original Documents…Commencing 1783*. Vol. 10, series 1. Philadelphia, PA: Joseph Severns & Company, 1854. Google e-book.

———. *Pennsylvania Archives: Selected and Arranged from Original Documents… Commencing 1790 with an Appendix*. Vol. 12, series 1. Philadelphia, PA: Joseph Severns & Company, 1856. Google e-book.

Herbert, Anne Hemphill. *Personal Memories of the Darlington Family at Guyasuta*. Pittsburgh, PA: University of Pittsburgh Press, 1949.

Lambing, A.A., Reverend. *A History of the Catholic Church in the Dioceses of Pittsburg and Allegheny from Its Establishment to the Present Time*. New York: Benziger Bros., 1880. Republished by University of Pittsburgh Digital Research Library, 1999. http://digital.library.pitt.edu/cgi-bin/t/text/text-idx?idno=00aga8651m;view=toc;c=pitttext.

Lyford, W.G. *The Western Address Directory*. Baltimore, MD: Jos. Robinson, 1837. Google e-book.

McClure, David. *Ohio Country Missionary: The Diary of David McClure, 1748–1820*. Waterville: Rettig's Frontier Ohio, 1996.

Michael Baker Jr. Inc. *Archeological Excavations in the Fort Pitt Block House, City of Pittsburgh, Allegheny County, Pennsylvania*. Moon Township, PA: Michael Baker Jr. Inc. Report given to the Fort Pitt Society of the Daughters of the American Revolution of Allegheny County, Pennsylvania, 2005.

Minutes of the Provincial Council of Pennsylvania, from the Organization to the Termination of the Proprietary Government. Vol. 10. Harrisburg, PA: Theo. Fenn & Company, 1852. Google e-book.

Muller, G.F. "The City of Pittsburgh." *Harper's New Monthly Magazine*, December 1880 to May 1881. Google e-book.

Pittsburgh Leader Almanac for 1872. Pittsburgh, PA: Pittock, Nevin & Company, 1872.

Stevens, Sylvester K., ed., et al. *The Papers of Henry Bouquet*. Vol. 2, *The Forbes Expedition*. Harrisburg: Pennsylvania Historical and Museum Commission, 1951.

Storey, Samuel. *To the Golden Land: Sketches of a Trip to Southern California*. London: Walter Scott, 1889. Google e-book.

Waddell, Louis M., ed., et al. *The Papers of Henry Bouquet*. Vol. 6, *Selected Documents, November 1761–July 1765 with a Catalog of Bouquet Papers from November 1761 to June 1767*. Harrisburg: Pennsylvania Historical and Museum Commission, 1994.

Watson, John F. *Annals of Philadelphia and Pennsylvania in the Olden Time*. Vol. 2. Philadelphia, PA: J.B. Lippincott & Company, 1870. Google e-book.

Westmoreland County Deed Book, vol. A. Westmoreland County Recorder of Deeds. http://www.wcdeeds.us/dts/Navigate.asp?SPVSearch.x=122&SPVSearch.y=18.

SECONDARY SOURCES

Alberts, Robert C. *The Shaping of the Point: Pittsburgh's Renaissance Park*. Pittsburgh, PA: University of Pittsburgh Press, 1980.

Anderson, Fred. *Crucible of War: The Seven Years' War and the Fate of Empire in British North America, 1754–1766*. New York: Vintage Books, 2000.

Baron, Stanley W. *Brewing in America: The History of Beer & Ale in the United States*. New York: Little, Brown & Company, 1962.

Boucher, John N., ed. *A Century and a Half of Pittsburgh and Her People*. Vol. 2. New York: Lewis Publishing Company, 1908. Google e-book.

Craig, Neville B. *The History of Pittsburgh*. Pittsburgh, PA: J.R. Weldin & Company, 1917.

Crytzer, Brady J. *Fort Pitt: A Frontier History*. Charleston, SC: The History Press, 2012.

Dahlinger, Charles. *Fort Pitt*. Pittsburgh, PA: privately printed, 1922.

Davis, Herman S., ed. *Reminiscences of General William Larimer and of His Son William H.H. Larimer, Two of the Founders of Denver City*. Pittsburgh, PA: privately printed by William Larimer Mellon, 1918. Google e-book.

Dixon, David. *Never Come to Peace Again: Pontiac's Uprising and the Fate of the British Empire in North America*. Norman: University of Oklahoma Press, 2005.

Dunnigan, Brian Leigh. *Forts Within a Fort: Niagara's Redoubts*. Youngstown, NY: Old Fort Niagara Association Inc., 1989.

Fleming, George T. *History of Pittsburgh and Environs.* Vol. 4. New York: American Historical Society, 1922. Google e-book.

Galloway, Edward A. "Guyasuta: Warrior, Estate & Home to the Boy Scouts." *Western Pennsylvania History Magazine* 94, no. 4 (Winter 2011–12).

James, Alfred Procter, and Charles Morse Stotz. *Drums in the Forest: Decision at the Forks, Defense in the Wilderness*. Pittsburgh, PA: University of Pittsburgh Press, 2005.

Jordan, John W. *Colonial and Revolutionary Families of Pennsylvania.* Vol. 3. New York: Lewis Publishing Company, 1911. Google e-book.

Linn, Kelly. "Patriotism Wins: The Story of the Pittsburgh Chapter of the DAR and Its Fight to Save the Fort Pitt Block House." Lecture given to the Pittsburgh Chapter of the NSDAR, September 8, 2010.

Nelson, Larry L. *A Man of Distinction Among Them: Alexander McKee and the Ohio Country Frontier, 1754–1799*. Kent, OH: Kent State University Press, 1999.

Pawlikowski, Melissah. "From the Bottom Up: Isaac Craig and the Process of Social and Economic Mobility During the Revolutionary Era." Master's thesis, Duquesne University, Pittsburgh, Pennsylvania, 2007.

Pittsburgh Places and Character-Building Words by Pittsburgh West Liberty Third-Grade Students. Pittsburgh, PA: Pittsburgh History & Landmarks Foundation, 2013.

Reed, George Irvine, ed. *Century Cyclopedia of History & Biography of Pennsylvania.* Vol. 2. Chicago, IL: Century Publishing & Engraving Company, 1904. Google e-book.

Salisbury, Ruth. "Pittsburgh's Great Romance." *Western Pennsylvania Historical Magazine* 47, no. 4 (October 1964): 343–54.

Shiras, George, III. *Justice George Shiras, Jr. of Pittsburgh: Chronicle of His Family, Life and Time*. Edited by Winfield Shiras. Pittsburgh, PA: University of Pittsburgh Press, 1953.

Stotz, Charles Morse. *Outposts of the War for Empire: The French and English in Western Pennsylvania: Their Armies, Their Forts, Their People, 1749–1764*. Pittsburgh, PA: University of Pittsburgh Press, 2005.

Water, Michael P. *Don't Call Me Boss: David L. Lawrence, Pittsburgh's Renaissance Mayor*. Pittsburgh, PA: University of Pittsburgh Press, 1988.

West, Patricia. *Domesticating History: The Political Origins of America's House Museums*. Washington, D.C.: Smithsonian Institution Press, 1999.

Williams, John S. *The American Pioneer.* Vol. 1. Cincinnati, OH: R.P. Brooks, 1842. Google e-book.

Websites

All Pittsburgh City Directory information was collected from Historic Pittsburgh, an online digitized library hosted by the University of Pittsburgh Digital Research Library. The Historic Pittsburgh site features digitized copies of almost every city directory for Pittsburgh from the mid-nineteenth century into the early twentieth century. Directories are digitized from the collections of the Senator John Heinz History Center and the Pittsburgh History & Landmarks Foundation. http://digital.library.pitt.edu/cgi-bin/t/text/text-idx?c=pitttextdir;page=browse;key=date.

Carnegie Library of Pittsburgh. "The Point: Living in the Block House." http://www.clpgh.org/exhibit/neighborhoods/point/point_n74.html.

The Darlington Digital Library, University of Pittsburgh. http://digital.library.pitt.edu/d/darlington/index.html.

Fort Pitt Block House. "Preservation & Restoration." Fort Pitt Block House, Fort Pitt Society of the Daughters of the American Revolution of Allegheny County, Pennsylvania. http://www.fortpittblockhouse.com/preservation-restoration.

McDonald, James. "Castle Architecture: Arrowslits or Loop-Holes." Castles and Manor Houses. http://www.castlesandmanorhouses.com/architecture.htm#loopholes.

National Park Service, Department of the Interior. "1768 Boundary Line Treaty of Fort Stanwix." Fort Stanwix National Monument. http://www.nps.gov/fost/historyculture/1768-boundary-line-treaty.htm.

Wagner, Holly. "Men from Early Middle Ages Were Nearly as Tall as Modern People." *Research News*, Ohio State University. http://researchnews.osu.edu/archive/medimen.htm.

Index

G

H

J

K

L

M

N

O

P

R

S

About the Author

Emily M. Weaver is the curator of the Fort Pitt Block House in Pittsburgh, a position she has held since June 2011. She received her Bachelor of Arts degree in history from Clarion University of Pennsylvania in 2009 and her Master of Arts degree in public history from Duquesne University in 2011. Prior to joining the Block House, Emily completed internships at several western Pennsylvania historical sites and organizations, including the Rivers of Steel National Heritage Area, the Oil Region Alliance and the Drake Well Museum. She served as a part-time instructor at Clarion University's Venango College in 2012, teaching courses on U.S. history. This book is her first published work. Emily currently resides in the Pittsburgh area with her husband, Jim.